COLLECTED POEMS

BY LAWRENCE DURRELL

COLLECTED POEMS

LAWRENCE DURRELL

E. P. DUTTON & CO., INC.
New York 1960

PREFACE

I HAVE arranged these poems, not according to chronology but in what I hope is the most easily readable form. Nothing has been included from the two earliest pamphlets. I date my poetic appearance from the publication of *A Private Country* in 1943.

Poems from the following volumes have been included: *Proems* edited by Oswell Blakeston (Fortune Press, 1938); *A Private Country* (Faber and Faber, 1943); *Cities, Plains and People* (Faber and Faber, 1946); *On Seeming to Presume* (Faber and Faber, 1948); *Sappho*: a play in verse (Faber and Faber, 1950); *The Tree of Idleness* (Faber and Faber, 1955); and *Private Drafts* (privately printed in Nicosia, Cyprus, 1955).

L.D.

CONTENTS

8

9

MNEIAE

Soft as puffs of smoke combining,
Mneiae—remembrance of past lives:

The shallow pigmentation of eternity
Upon the pouch of time and place existing.

I, the watcher, smoking at a table,
And I, my selves, observed by human choice,

A disinherited portion of the whole:
With you the sibling of my self-desire,

The carnal and the temporal voice,
The singing bird upon the spire:

And love, the grammar of that war
Which time's the only ointment for,

Which time's the only ointment for.

LESBOS

The Pleiades are sinking calm as paint,
And earth's huge camber follows out,
Turning in sleep, the oceanic curve,

Defined in concave like a human eye
Or cheek pressed warm on the dark's cheek,
Like dancers to a music they deserve.

This balcony, a moon-anointed shelf
Above a silent garden holds my bed.
I slept. But the dispiriting autumn moon,

In her slow expurgation of the sky
Needs company: is brooding on the dead,
And so am I now, so am I.

WATER MUSIC

Wrap your sulky beauty up,
From sea-fever, from winterfall
Out of the swing of the
Swing of the sea.

Keep safe from noonfall,
Starlight and smokefall where
Waves roll, waves toll but feel
None of our roving fever.

From dayfever and nightsadness
Keep, bless, hold: from cold
Wrap your sulky beauty into sleep
Out of the swing of the
Swing of sea.

NEMEA

A song in the valley of Nemea:
Sing quiet, quite quiet here.

Song for the brides of Argos
Combing the swarms of golden hair:
Quite quiet, quiet there.

Under the rolling comb of grass,
The sword outrusts the golden helm.

Agamemnon under tumulus serene
Outsmiles the jury of skeletons:
Cool under cumulus the lion queen:

Only the drum can celebrate,
Only the adjective outlive them.

A song in the valley of Nemea:
Sing quiet, quiet, quiet here.

Tone of the frog in the empty well,
Drone of the bald bee on the cold skull,

Quiet, Quiet, Quiet.

ORPHEUS

Orpheus, beloved famulus,
Know to us in a dark congeries
Of intimations from the dead:
Encamping among our verses—
Harp-beats of a sea-bird's wings—
Do you contend in us, though now
A memory only, the smashed lyre
Washed up entangled in your hair,
But sounding still as here,
O monarch of all initiates and
The dancer's only perfect peer?

In the fecund silences of the
Painter, or the poet's wrestling
With choice you steer like
A great albatross, spread white
On the earth-margins the sailing
Snow-wings in the world's afterlight:
Mentor of all these paper ships
Cockled from fancy on a tide
Made navigable only by your skill
Which in some few approves
A paper recreation of lost loves.

STYLE

Something like the sea,
Unlaboured momentum of water
But going somewhere,
Building and subsiding,
The busy one, the loveless.

Or the wind that slits
Forests from end to end,
Inspiriting vast audiences,
Ovations of leafy hands
Accepting, accepting.

But neither is yet
Fine enough for the line I hunt.
The dry bony blade of the
Sword-grass might suit me
Better: an assassin of polish.

Such a bite of perfect temper
As unwary fingers provoke,
Not to be felt till later,
Turning away, to notice the thread
Of blood from its unfelt stroke.

CHANEL

Scent like a river-pilot led me there:
Bedroom darkness spreading like a moss,
The polished wells of floors in blackness
Gave no reflections of the personage,
Or the half-open door, but whispered on:

'Skin be supple, hair be smooth,
Lips and character attend
In mnemonic solitude.
Kisses leave no fingerprints.'
'Answer.' But no answer came.
'Beauty hunted leaves no clues.'

Yet as if rising from a still,
Perfume whispered at the sill,
All those discarded husks of thought
Hanging untenanted like gowns,
Rinds of which the fruit had gone . . .

Still the long chapter led me on.
Still the clock beside the bed
Heart-beat after heart-beat shed.

NIKI

Love on a leave-of-absence came,
Unmoored the silence like a barge,
Set free to float on lagging webs
The swan-black wise unhindered night.

(Bitter and pathless were the ways
Of sleep to which such beauty led.)

THIS UNIMPORTANT MORNING

This unimportant morning
Something goes singing where
The capes turn over on their sides
And the warm Adriatic rides
Her blue and sun washing
At the edge of the world and its brilliant cliffs.

Day rings in the higher airs
Pure with cicadas, and slowing
Like a pulse to smoke from farms,
Extinguished in the exhausted earth,
Unclenching like a fist and going.

Trees fume, cool, pour—and overflowing
Unstretch the feathers of birds and shake
Carpets from windows, brush with dew
The up-and-doing: and young lovers now
Their little resurrections make.

And now lightly to kiss all whom sleep
Stitched up—and wake, my darling, wake.
The impatient Boatman has been waiting
Under the house, his long oars folded up
Like wings in waiting on the darkling lake.

THE DYING FALL

The islands rebuffed by water.
Estuaries of putty and gold.
A smokeless arc of Latin sky.
One star, less than a week old.

Memory now, I lead her haltered.
Stab of the opiate in the arm
When the sea wears bronze scales and
Hushes in the ambush of a calm.

The old dialogue always rebegins
Between us: but now the spring
Ripens, neither will be attending,
For rosy as feet of pigeons pressed

In clay, the kisses we possessed,
Or thought we did: so borrowing, lending,
Stacked fortunes in our love's society—
Each in the perfect circle of a sigh was ending.

PATMOS

Early one morning unremarked
She walked abroad to see
Black bitumen and roses
Upon the island shelf
To hear those inexperienced
Thrushes repeat their clauses
From some corruptible tree
All copied in herself.

When from the Grecian meadows
Responsive rose the larks,
Stiffly as if on strings,
Ebbing, drew thin as tops
While each in rising squeezed
His spire of singing drops
On that renewed landscape
Like semen from the grape.

GREEN MAN

Four small nouns I put to pasture,
Lambs of cloud on a green paper.
My love leans like a beadle at her book,
Her smile washes the seven cities.

I am the spring's greenest publicity,
And my poem is all wrist and elbow.
O I am not daedal and need wings,
My oracle kisses a black wand.

One great verb I dip in ink
For the tortoise who carries the earth:
A grammar of fate like the map of China,
Or as wrinkles sit in the palm of a girl.

I enter my poem like a son's house.
The ancient thought is: nothing will change.
But the nouns are back in the bottle,
I ache and she is warm, was warm, is warm.

POEM

Find time hanging, cut it down
All the universe you own.

Masterless and still untamed
Poet, lead the race you've shamed.

Lover, cut the rational knot
That made your thinking rule-of-thumb

And barefoot on the plum-dark hills
Go Wander in Elysium.

LINES TO MUSIC

Ride out at midnight,
You will meet your sun.
Into what arsenal now seem fallen
The germs of the plum and the peppercorn?
The born and the unborn will report
What poison licks the wheat,
Or in the melon's gold retort
Repeat what melody fattens the leopard
From his mother's dusky teat.

Ride out at midnight
And number the sparrows.
Who put great wings to the Ark?
Who gave the unicorn spurs?
Only the women with thighs like mackerel,
Nourish the germ of the man of sorrows,
Are true to their monsters.
Be you to yours.

THE PILOT

To Dudley Honor

Sure a lovely day and all weather
Leading westward to Ireland and our childhood.
On the quarters of heaven, held by stars,
The Hunter and Arcturus getting ready—
The elect of heaven all burning on the wheel.

This lovely morning must the pilot leaning
In the eye of heaven feel the island
Turning beneath him, burning soft and blue—
And all this mortal globe like a great lamp
With spines of rivers, families of cities
Seeming to the solitary boy so
Local and queer yet so much part of him.

The enemies of silence have come nearer.
Turn, turn to the morning on wild elbows:
Look down through the five senses like stars
To where our lives lie small and equal like two grains
Before Chance—the hawk's eye or the pilot's
Round and shining on the open sky,
Reflecting back the innocent world in it.

LOGOS

Thy kingdom come. They say the prophet
In private house lies with his myth:
Sees strange particularities in flesh
That poison his beatitude.

Onlie begetter, shining one
We travel a same rare latitude
To fringe the Arctic Circle of the Word:
Carry no compass, flag to plant, but bone.
The ageless humour of the skeleton.

His myth is grace: no less our absolute,
Locust and honey, scrip and wallet. Woman
Can be a wilderness enough for body
To wander in: is a true human
Genesis and exodus. A serious fate.

She the last crucifixion on the Word.
We press on her as Roman on his sword.

THE COTTAGER

Here is a man who says: Let there be light.
Let who is dressed in hair walk upright,
The house give black smoke, the children
Be silenced by fire and apples. Let
A sedative evening bring steaming cattle
The domestic kettle, contagion of sleep,
Deeper purer surer even than Eden.
Twin tides speak making of two three
By fission by fusion, a logarithmic sea.

What was bitter in the apple is eaten deep,
Rust sleeps in the steel, canker will keep.
Let one plus one quicken and be two,
Keep silence that silence keep you.

THE POET

Time marched against my egg,
But Saturn hatched it:
Furnished two rusty claws,
The antelope's logic:
While by the turtle's coma in summer
The new moon watched it.

Four seasons conspired
To poison my water: with scissors
A late spring lanced the bud,
Tightened the caul on my skull,
Lulled me in dragon's blood.

Sun withered this crucible head,
Wove me by a tragical loom.
Nine moons heard of my coming,
The drumming of mythical horses
On the walls of the womb.

Winter buried the eyes like talents.
Tightened the temple's bony ring,
And now the pie is opened,
Feathered the head of the owlet—
What shall the monster sing?

BERE REGIS

The colonial, the expatriate walking here
Awkwardly enclosing the commonwealth of his love
Stoops to this lovely expurgated prose-land
Where winter with its holly locks the schools
And spring with nature improvises
With the thrush on ploughland, with the scarecrow.

Moss walls, woollen forests, Shakespear, desuetude:
Roots of his language as familiar as salt
Inhaling cattle lick in this mnemonic valley
Where the gnats assort, the thrush familiarises,
And over his cottage a colloquial moon.

PEARLS

Now mark, the Lady one fine day
To refresh her pearls she comes
And buries them in the sand here,
Letting the sea feed on them,
To lick back by salt
The lustre of them and the prize.

Ten summers, lazy as fishes follow.
Ten winters, nude as thimbles
Bear on their gradual curves
The drinkers of the darkness.

The pearls drink and recover
But their lovely Neck
Becomes one day the target for an Axe,
Bows swan-like down
Its unrepenting lovely stump.

Something is incomplete here,
Something in the story is unfinished,
A tale with no beginning,
The fragment of a voice that interrupts,
Like this unbroken coast,
Like this half-drawn landscape,
Like this broken torso of a poem.

A PROSPECT OF CHILDREN

All summer watch the children in the public garden,
The tribe of children wishing you were like them—
These gruesome little artists of the impulse
For whom the perfect anarchy sustains
A brilliant apprehension of the present,
In games of joy, of love or even murder
On this green springing grass will empty soon
A duller opiate, Loving, to the drains.

Cast down like asterisks among their toys,
Divided by the lines of daylight only
From adventure, crawl among the rocking-horses,
And the totems, dolls and animals and rings
To the tame suffix of a nursery sleep
Where all but few of them
The restless inventories of feeling keep.

Sleep has no walls. Sleep admits
The great Imago with its terror, yet they lie
Like something baking, candid cheek on finger,
With folded lip and eye
Each at the centre of the cobweb seeking
His boy or girl, begotten and confined
In terror like the edges of a table
Begot by passion and confirmed in error.

What can they tell the watcher at the window,
Writing letters, smoking up there alone,
Trapped in the same limitation of his growth
And yet not envying them their childhood
Since he endured his own?

FOR A NURSERY MIRROR

Image, Image, Image answer
Whether son or whether daughter,
The persuader or the dancer:
A bird's beak poking out of the flesh,
A bird's beak singing between the eyes.

'The earth is a loaf,
Image, Image, Image,
The wet part is joined to the dry,
Like the joints of Adam.'

It is dark now. Rise.
Between the Nonself and the Self
Cover the little wound
With soft red clay,
From the hit of the wind of Death,
From the chink of the pin of Day.

The heart's cold singing part,
Image of the Dancer in water,
Close up with the soft red clay
The wound in the mystical bud:
For the dancers walking in the water
This is the body, this the blood.

TO PING-KÛ, ASLEEP

You sleeping child asleep, away
Between the confusing world of forms,
The lamplight and the day; you lie
And the pause flows through you like glass,
Asleep in the body of the nautilus.

Between comparison and sleep,
Lips that move in quotation;
The turning of a small blind mind
Like a plant everywhere ascending.
Now our love has become a beanstalk.

Invent a language where the terms
Are smiles; someone in the house now
Only understands warmth and cherish,
Still twig-bound, learning to fly.

This hand exploring the world makes
The diver's deep-sea fingers on the sills
of underwater windows; all the wrecks
Of our world where the sad blood leads back
Through memory and sense like divers working.

Sleep, my dear, we won't disturb
You, lying in the zones of sleep.
The four walls symbolise love put about
To hold in silence which so soon brims
Over into sadness: it's still dark.

Sleep and rise a lady with a flower
Between your teeth and a cypress
Between your thighs: surely you won't ever
Be puzzled by a poem or disturbed by a poem
Made like fire by the rubbing of two sticks?

ON SEEMING TO PRESUME

On seeming to presume
Where earth and water plan
No place for him, no home
Outside the confining womb,
Mistake him if you can.
The rubber forceps do their job
And here at last stands man.

Refined by no technique
Beyond the great 'I will',
They pour the poison in,
Confuse the middle ear
Of his tormented dust,
Before the brute can speak
'I will' becomes 'I must'.

Excluded from the true
Participating love
His conscience takes its due
From this excluding sense
His condemnation brought.
From past to future tense
He mutters on 'I ought'.

He mutters on 'I ought'.

Yet daring to presume
He follows to the stews
His sense of loathsomeness,
Frustration, daily news.

A scholarship in hate
Endows him limb by limb.
'My mother pushed me from behind,
And so I learned to swim.'

The bunsen's head of hair,
All fancy free and passion,
Till iron circumstance
Confirms him in his lies,
To walk the Hamlet fashion.
He wrings his hands and cries
'I want to live', but dies.

He wants to live but dies.

Return, return and find
Beneath what bed or table
The lovers first in mind
Composed this poor unstable
Derivative of clay,
By passion or by play,
That bears the human label.

What king or saint could guide
This caliban of gloom
So swaddled in despair
To breathe the factory's air,
Or locked in furnished room
Weep out his threescore there
For seeming to presume,

For seeming to presume?

CRADLE SONG

Erce . . . Erce . . . Erce
Primigravida

curled like a hoop in sleep
unearthly of manufacture,
tissue of blossom and clay
bone the extract of air
fountain of nature.

softly knitted by kisses,
added to stitch by stitch,
by sleep of the dying heart,
by water and wool and air,
gather a fabric rich.

earth contracted to earth
in ten toes: the cardinals.
in ten fingers: the bishops.
ears by two, eyes by two,
watch the mirror watching you,

and now hush

the nightwalkers bringing peace,
seven the badges of grace
five the straw caps of talent,
one the scarf of desire, go
mimic your mother's lovely face.

RIVER WATER

The forest wears its coats
of oil-paint as lightly can
what only brush-strokes built,
feather and leaf and spray,
married by choice and plan.

Curve of the Danube's wrist
leans from its mossy bed,
takes the bias of earth with it
the camber of earth and sky,
divides with a ruler of lead.

Soft as an ant's patrol
fingers to fingers warm,
to relive in a favourite's touch,
warm as the oven-loaf,
to finger and wrist and arm.

We know that the dead forget:
the living reside in touch,
sweet consonance of a kiss,
or a letter from distant home,
says little and yet so much.

So much yet never enough
in the concert of night and day,
but revisit us like the dead
kisses that rise to our lips
confused in the river's spray.

Dead kisses revisit the living
in guises our bodies abet,
for mouth or elbow or thigh:
for the living must always remember
what the dead can never forget.

SONG

Proffer the loaves of pain
Forward and back again,
By time's inflexible quantum
They shall not meet this autumn.

Stone islets, stars in stations,
Crab up their false equations,
Whether they run or saunter
They shall not meet this winter.

Boredom of breathless swan
Whiteness they gazed upon,
At skylight a roamer.
They shall not meet in summer.

Fast on these capes of green
Silence falls in between
Finger and wedding-ring.
They shall not meet in spring.

THE OCTAGON ROOM

Veronese grey! Here in the Octagon Room
Our light ruffles and decodes
Greys of cigar-ash or river clay
Into the textual plumage of a mind—
Paulo, all his Muses held
Quietly in emulsion up against
A pane of cockney sky.

It is not only the authority
Of godly sensual forms which pity
And overwhelm us—this grey copied
From eyes I no more see,
Recording every shade of pain, yes,
All it takes to give smiles
The deathly candour of a dying art,
Or worth to words exchanged in darkness:
Is it only the dead who have such eyes?

No, really,
I think it is the feudal calm
Of sensuality enjoyed without aversion
Or regret . . . (incident of the ring
Lost in the grass: her laughter).

I should have been happy
In these rainy streets, a captive still
Like all these glittering hostages
We carried out of Italy, canvases
Riding the cracking winds in great London
Parks: happy or unhappy, who can tell you?

Only Veronese grey walks backwards
In the past across my mind
To where tugs still howl and mumble
On the father river,
And the grey feet passing, quiver
On pavements greyer than his greys . . .

Less wounding perhaps because the belongers
Loved here, died here, and took their art
Like love, with a pinch of salt, yes
Their pain clutched in the speechless
Deathless calm of Method. Gods!

POMONA DE MAILLOL

An old man tamed his garden with wet clay
Until Pomona rose, a bubble in his arms.

The time and place grow ripe when the idea
Marries its proper image in volition,
When desire and intention kiss and bruise.

A cord passed round the body of the mermaid
Drew her sleeping from the underworld,
As when the breath of resin like a code
Rises from some unguarded still, Pomona
Breathing, surely a little out of breath
The image disengaging from the block,
A little out of breath, and wondering

If art is self-reflection, *who* he was
She woke within the side of, *what* old man
In his smock and dirty cap of cloth,
Drinking through trembling fingers now
A ten year siege of her, the joy in touching
The moistened flanks of her idea with all
An old man's impatience of the carnal wish?

'JE EST UN AUTRE'
—Rimbaud

He is the man who makes notes,
The observer in the tall black hat,
Face hidden in the brim:
In three European cities
He has watched me watching him.

The street-corner in Buda and after
By the post-office a glimpse
Of the disappearing tails of his coat,
Gave the same illumination, spied upon,
The tightness in the throat.

Once too meeting by the Seine
The waters a moving floor of stars,
He had vanished when I reached the door,
But there on the pavement burning
Lay one of his familiar black cigars.

The meeting on the dark stairway
Where the tide ran clean as a loom:
The betrayal of her, her kisses
He has witnessed them all: often
I hear him laughing in the other room.

He watches me now, working late,
Bringing a poem to life, his eyes
Reflect the malady of De Nerval:
O useless in this old house to question
The mirrors, his impenetrable disguise.

NIGHT EXPRESS

Night falls. The dark expresses
Roll back their iron scissors to commence
Precision of the wheels' elision
From whose dark serial jabber sparks
Swing swaying through the mournful capitals

And in these lighted cages sleep
With open eyes the passengers
Each committed to his private folly,
On hinges of wanhope the long
Sleeping shelves of men and women,
A library of maggots dreaming, rolls.

Some retiring to their sleeping past,
On clicking pillows feel the flickering peep
Of lighted memories, keys slipped in groves
Parted like lips receiving or resisting kisses.
Pillars of smoke expend futurity.

This is how it is for me, for you
It must be different lying awake to hear
At a garden's end the terrible club-foot
Crashing among iron spars, the female shrieks,
Love-song of steel and the consenting night.

To feel the mocking janitor, sleep,
Shake now and wake to lean there
On a soft elbow seeing where we race
A whiplash curving outwards to the stars,
A glowing coal to light the lamps of space.

SWANS

Fraudulent perhaps in that they gave
No sense of muscle but a swollen languor
Though moved by webs: yet idly, idly
As soap-bubbles drift from a clay-pipe
They mowed the lake in tapestry,

Passing in regal exhaustion by us,
King, queen and cygnets, one by one.
Did one dare to remember other swans
In anecdotes of Gauguin or of Rabelais?
Some became bolsters for the Greeks,
Some rubber Lohengrins provided comedy.
The flapping of the wings excited Leda.
The procession is over and what is now
Alarming is more the mirror split
From end to end by the harsh clap
Of the wooden beaks, than the empty space
Which follows them about,
Stained by their whiteness when they pass.

We sit like drunkards and inhale the swans.

AT STRATI'S

Remember please, time has no joints,
Pours over the great sills of thought,
Not clogging nor resisting but
Yawning to inherit the year's quarters;
Weaving you up the unbroken series
Of corn, ammonites and men
In a single unlaboured continuum,
And not in slices called by day and night,
And not in objects called by place and thing.

You say I do not write, but the taverns
Have no clocks, and I conscripted
By loneliness observe how other drinkers
Sit at Strati's embalmed in reverie:
Forms raise green cones of wine,
And loaded heads recline on loaded arms,
Under a sky pronounced by cypresses,
Packed up, all of us, like loaves
Human and plant, memory and wish.

The very calendar props an empty inkwell.

EDUCATION OF A CLOUD

You saw them, Sabina? Did you see them?
Yet the education of this little cloud
Full of neglect, allowed remissly so to lie
Unbrushed in some forgotten corner
Of a Monday-afternoon-in-April sky . . .

The rest abandoned it in passing by,
The swollen red-eyed country-mourners,
Unbarbered, marching on some Friday-the-thirteenth.
They knew it was not of the savage
Winter company, this tuffet for a tired cherub,

But a dear belonging of the vernal age,
Say spring, provinces of the nightingale,
Say love, the ministry of all distresses,
Say youth, Sabina, let us call it youth—

All the white capes of fancy seen afar!

THE TREE OF IDLENESS

I shall die one day I suppose
In this old Turkish house I inhabit:
A ragged banana-leaf outside and here
On the sill in a jam-jar a rock-rose.

Perhaps a single pining mandolin
Throbs where cicadas have quarried
To the heart of all misgiving and there
Scratches on silence like a pet locked in.

Will I be more or less dead
Than the village in memory's dispersing
Springs, or in some cloud of witness see,
Looking back, the selfsame road ahead?

By the moist clay of a woman's wanting,
After the heart has stopped its fearful
Gnawing, will I descry between
This life and that another sort of haunting?

No: the card-players in tabs of shade
Will play on: the aerial springs
Hiss: in bed lying quiet under kisses
Without signature, with all my debts unpaid

I shall recall nights of squinting rain,
Like pig-iron on the hills: bruised
Landscapes of drumming cloud and everywhere
The lack of someone spreading like a stain.

Or where brown fingers in the darkness move,
Before the early shepherds have awoken,
Tap out on sleeping lips with these same
Worn typewriter keys a poem imploring

Silence of lips and minds which have not spoken.

THE SIRENS

Trembling they appear, the Siren isles,
Bequeathing lavender and molten rose,

Reflecting in the white caves of our sails
Melodious capes of fancy and of terror,

Where now the singers surface at the prow,
Begin the famous, pitiless, wounded singing . . .

Ulysses watching, like many a hero since,
Thinks: 'Voyages and privations!

The loutish sea which swallows up our loves,
Lying windless under a sky of lilac,

Far from our home, the longed-for landfall . . .
By God! They choose their time, the Sirens.'

Every poet and hero has to face them,
The glittering temptresses of his distraction,

The penalties which seek him for a hostage.
Homer and Milton: both were punished in their gift.

ON MIRRORS

You gone, the mirrors all reverted,
Lay banging in the empty house,
Redoubled their efforts to impede
Waterlogged images of faces pleading.

So Fortunatus had a mirror which
Imperilled his reason when it broke;
The sleepers in their dormitory of glass
Stirred once and sighed but never woke.

Time amputated so will bleed no more
But flow like refuse now in clocks
On clinic walls, in libraries and barracks,
Not made to spend but kill and nothing more.

Yet mirrors abandoned drink like ponds:
(Once they resumed the childhood of love)
And overflowing, spreading, swallowing
Like water light, show one averted face,

As in the capsule of the human eye
Seen at infinity, the outer end of time,
A man and woman lying sun-bemused
In a blue vineyard by the Latin sea,

Steeped in each other's minds and breathing there
Like wicks inhaling deep in golden oil.

A BOWL OF ROSES

'Spring' says your Alexandrian poet
'Means time of the remission of the rose'

Now here at this tattered old café,
By the sea-wall, where so many like us
Have felt the revengeful power of life,
Are roses trapped in blue tin bowls.
I think of you somewhere among them—
Other roses—outworn by our literature,
Made tenants of calf-love or else
The poet's portion, a black black rose
Coughed into the helpless lap of love,
Or fallen from a lapel—a night-club rose.

It would take more than this loving imagination
To claim them for you out of time,
To make them dense and fecund so that
Snow would never pocket them, nor would
They travel under glass to great sanatoria
And like a sibling of the sickness thrust
Flushed faces up beside a dead man's plate.

No, you should have picked one from a poem
Being written softly with a brush—
The deathless ideogram for love we writers hunt.
Now alas the writing and the roses, Melissa,
Are nearly over: who will next remember
Their spring remission in kept promises,

Or even the true ground of their invention
In some dry heart or earthen inkwell?

AT THE LONG BAR

Bowed like a foetus at the long bar sit,
You common artist whose uncommon ends
Deflower the secret contours of a mind
And all around you pitying find
Like severed veins your earthly friends . . .

(*The sickness of the oyster is the pearl*)

Dead bottles all around infect
Stale air the exploding corks bewitch—
O member of this outlawed sect,
Only the intolerable itch,
Skirt-fever, keeps the anthropoid erect.

Husband or wife or child condemn
This chain-gang which we all inherit:
Or those bleak ladders to despair
Miscalled high place and merit.
Dear, if these knotted words could wake
The dead boy and the buried girl. . . .

(*The sickness of the oyster is the pearl*)

BITTER LEMONS

In an island of bitter lemons
Where the moon's cool fevers burn
From the dark globes of the fruit,

And the dry grass underfoot
Tortures memory and revises
Habits half a lifetime dead

Better leave the rest unsaid,
Beauty, darkness, vehemence
Let the old sea-nurses keep

Their memorials of sleep
And the Greek sea's curly head
Keep its calms like tears unshed

Keep its calms like tears unshed.

CLOUDS OF GLORY

The baby emperor,
reigning on tuffet, throne or pot
in his minority knows hardly what
    he is, or is not,
     sagely he confers
his card of humours like a vane,
veering by fair to jungle foul
    so shapes his course
through variable back to fine again.

    Then
fingers dangle over him: beanstalks.
chins like balconies impend:
kisses like blank thunder bang
    above the little mandarin,
or like a precious ointment prest
from tubes are different kisses
    to the suffrage of a grin.

    He can outface
a hundred generations with a yawn
    this Faustus of the pram,
spreadeagled like a starfish, or
    some uncooked prawn
with pink and toothless mandible
    advance the proposition:
     'I
    cry, therefore I am'

    the baby emperor
    O lastly see
in exile on his favourite St. Helena,

corner of a lost playground gazing
    into a dark well,
manufacturing images of a lost past,
expense of spirit in a waste of longing,
    sea-nymphs hourly
    ring his knell.

    small famulus of Time!
born to the legation of our dark unknowing
    the seed was not your
sowing, nor did you make these tall
    untoppled walls
to sit here like a prisoner remembering
    only as a poem now
    the past, the white breasts
that once leaned over you like waterfalls.

NOTEBOOK

Mothers and sculptors work
By small rehearsed caresses in the block
Each to redeeming ends,
By shame or kisses print
Good citizens, good lovers and good friends.

Your impatient hero so admired
In all his epic scenery
Was such a vessel once, unfired,
A chaos on the wheel and rocked
In a muse on the womb's dark Galilee.

And the lovers, those two characters,
Who have their exits and their entrances,
A certain native style may give
As predetermined in the bone,
Speak through the crude gags of the grave.

Their luck and hazard rests, my dear,
So lightly on us in our dreams
As voices rich with tears,
Whom no poetic justice gave
A friendship mad as ours.

MAREOTIS

For Diana Gould

Now everywhere Spring opens
Like an eyelid still unfocused,
Unsharpened in expression yet or depth,
But smiling and entire, stirring from sleep.

Birds begin, swindlers of the morning.
Flowers and the wild ways begin:
And the body's navigation in its love
Through wings, messages, telegrams
Loose and unbodied roam the world.

Only we are held here on the
Rationed love—a landscape like an eye,
Where the wind gnashes by Mareotis,
Stiffens the reeds and glistening salt,
And in the ancient roads the wind,
Not subtle, not confiding, touches once again
The melancholy elbow cheek and paper.

DELOS

For Diana Gould

On charts they fall like lace,
Islands consuming in a sea
Born dense with its own blue:
And like repairing mirrors holding up
Small towns and trees and rivers
To the still air, the lovely air:
From the clear side of springing Time,
In clement places where the windmills ride,
Turning over grey springs in Mykonos,
In shadows with a gesture of content.

The statues of the dead here
Embark on sunlight, sealed
Each in her model with the sightless eyes:
The modest stones of Greeks,
Who gravely interrupted death by pleasure.

And in harbours softly fallen
The liver-coloured sails—
Sharp-featured brigantines with eyes—
Ride in reception so like women:
The pathetic faculty of girls
To register and utter a desire
In the arms of men upon the new-mown waters,
Follow the wind, with their long shining keels
Aimed across Delos at a star.

.
t bone break
f a poem holds on,
her
her have done.

strokes,
s, glance the bare bone
verve I quicken,
ly's prime carbon,

rees speak and doves
the pith of the planet
, status of music: God
, memory, aftermath

r love lessens,
poem lives on
weather
have gone.

PHILEREMO

A philosopher in search of human values
Might have seen something in the coarse
Black boots the guide wore when he led us:
Boots with cracked eyes and introspective
Laces, rich in historical error as this
Old wall we picked the moss from, reading
Into it invasions by the Dorians or Medes.

But the bearded arboreal historian
Saw nothing of it all, was nothing then.
His education had derailed the man
Until he moved, a literary reminiscence,
Through quotations only, fine as hair.

The stones spoke to him. Reflected there
In a cistern I heard you thinking: Europe
Also, the whole of our egopetal culture
Is done for and must vanish soon.

And still we have not undergone the poet's truth.

Could he comfort us in more than this
Blue sea and air cohering blandly
Across that haze of flats,
The smoking middens of our history—
Aware perhaps only of the two children
Asleep in the car beside a bear in cotton gloves?

At insular café tables under awnings
Bemused benighted half-castes pause
To stretch upon a table yawning
Ten yellow claws and
Order green coconuts to drink with straws.

Milk of the green loaf-coconuts
Which soon before them amputated stand,
Broken, you think, from some great tree of breasts
Or the green skulls of savages trepanned.

Lips that are curved to taste this albumen,
To dredge with some blue spoon among the cur
Which drying on tongue or on moustache are ta
As droppings of bats or birds.

Re-enacting here a theory out of Darwin
They cup their yellow mandibles to shape
Their nuts, tilt them in drinking posts,
To drain them slowly from the very nape:
Green coconuts, green
Coconuts, patrimony of the ape.

I, per se I, I sing o
Let flesh falter, or l
Break, yet the salt
Even in empty weat
When beak and feat

I am such fiddle-glib
As play on the nerve
With the madman's
Leaven and liven bod
I, per se I, alone.

This is my medicine:
Talk, woods walk: in
Is undertone, overton
Opens each fent, scen
In the sky and the so

O per se O, I sing on.
Never tongue falters o
Lessens. The salt of th
Like this carol of empt
Now feather and beak

BLIND HOMER

A winter night again, and the moon
Loosely inks in the marbles and retires.

The six pines whistle and stretch and there,
Eastward the loaded brush of morning pauses

Where the few Grecian stars sink and revive
Each night in glittering baths of sound.

Now to the winter each has given up
Deciduous stuff, the snakeskin and the antler,

Cast skin of poetry and the grape.

Blind Homer, the lizards still sup the heat
From the rocks, and still the spring,

Noiseless as coins on hair repeats
Her diphthong after diphthong endlessly.

Exchange a glance with one whose art
Conspires with introspection against loneliness

This February 1946, pulse normal, nerves at rest:
Heir to a like disorder, only lately grown

Much more uncertain of his gift with words,
By this plate of olives, this dry inkwell.

THE LOST CITIES

For Paddy and Xan

One she floats as Venice might,
Bloated among her ambiguities:
What hebetude or carelessness shored up
Goths were not smart enough to capture.
The city, yes: the water: not the style.

Her dispossession now may seem to us
Idle and ridiculous, quivering
in the swollen woodwork of these
Floating carcases of the doges,
Dissolving into spires and cages of water:
Venice blown up, and turning green.

Another wears out humbly like a craft:
Red wells where the potter's thumb
Sealed his jars of guaranteed oil.
That fluent thumb which presses
On history's vibrating string,
Pressing here, there, in a wounded place.

Some have left names only: Carthage:
Where the traveller may squeeze out
A few drops of ink or salt,
On deserted promontories may think:
'No wonder. A river once turned over
In its sleep and all the cities fled.'

Now in Greece which is not yet Greece
The adversary was also strong.
Yet here the serfs have built their discontents
As spiders do their junctions, here,

This orchard, painted tables set outside
A whitewashed house,
And on a rusty nail the violin
Is hanging by one wrist, still ownerless:

Disowned by the devastator and as yet
Uncherished by its tenants in the old
Human smells of excrement and cooking:
Waiting till the spades press through to us,
To be discovered, standing in our lives,

Rhodes, death-mask of a Greek town.

LEVANT

Gum, oats and syrup
The Arabians bore.
Evoking nothing from the sea but more
And more employ to christen them
With whips of salt and glittering spray,
Their wooden homes rocked on the chastening salt.

Lamps on altars, breath of children;
So coming and going with their talk of bales,
Lading and enterprises marked out
And fell on this rusty harbour
Where tills grew fat with cash
And the quills of Jews invented credit,
And in margins folded up
Bales, gum-arabic, and syrup;
Syrian barley in biffed coracles
Hugging the burking gulf or blown
As cargoes from the viny breath
Of mariners, the English or the Dutch.
In manners taught them nothing much
Beyond the endurance in the vile.
Left in history words like
Portuguese or Greek
Whose bastards can still speak and smile.

After this, lamps
Confused the foreigners;
Boys, women and drugs
Built this ant-hill for grammarians
Who fed upon the fathers fat with cash,

Turned oats and syrup here
To ribbons and wands and rash
Patents for sex and feathers,
Sweets for festivals and deaths.

Nothing changes. The indifferent
Or the merely good died off, but fixed
Here once the human type 'Levant'.
Something fine of tooth and with the soft
Hanging lashes to the eye,
Given once by Spain and kept
In a mad friendship here and sadness
By the promiscuous sea upon this spit of sand.

Something money or promises can buy.

ALEXANDRIA

To the lucky now who have lovers or friends,
Who move to their sweet undiscovered ends,
Or whom the great conspiracy deceives,
I wish these whirling autumn leaves:
Promontories splashed by the salty sea,
Groaned on in darkness by the tram
To horizons of love or good luck or more love—
As for me I now move
Through many negatives to what I am.

Here at the last cold Pharos between Greece
And all I love, the lights confide
A deeper darkness to the rubbing tide;
Doors shut, and we the living are locked inside
Between the shadows and the thoughts of peace:
And so in furnished rooms revise
The index of our lovers and our friends
From gestures possibly forgotten, but the ends
Of longings like unconnected nerves,
And in this quiet rehearsal of their acts
We dream of them and cherish them as Facts.

Now when the sea grows restless as a conscript,
Excited by fresh wind, climbs the sea-wall,
I walk by it and think about you all:
B. with his respect for the Object, and D.
Searching in sex like a great pantry for jars
Marked 'Plum and apple'; and the small, fell
Figure of Dorian ringing like a muffin-bell—
All indeed whom war or time threw up
On this littoral and tides could not move
Were objects for my study and my love.

And then turning where the last pale
Lighthouse, like a Samson blinded, stands
And turns its huge charred orbit on the sands
I think of you—indeed mostly of you,
In whom a writer would only name and lose
The dented boy's lip and the close
Archer's shoulders; but here to rediscover
By tides and faults of weather, by the rain
Which washes everything, the critic and the lover.

At the doors of Africa so many towns founded
Upon a parting could become Alexandria, like
The wife of Lot—a metaphor for tears;
And the queer student in his poky hot
Tenth floor room above the harbour hears
The sirens shaking the tree of his heart,
And shuts his books, while the most
Inexpressible longings like wounds unstitched
Stir in him some girl's unquiet ghost.

So we, learning to suffer and not condemn
Can only wish you this great pure wind
Condemned by Greece, and turning like a helm
Inland where it smokes the fires of men,
Spins weathercocks on farms or catches
The lovers at their quarrel in the sheets;
Or like a walker in the darkness might,
Knocks and disturbs the artist at his papers
Up there alone, upon the alps of night.

RODINI

Windless plane-trees above Rodini
To the pencil or the eye are tempters

Where of late trees have become ears in leaf
Curved for the cicada's first monotony

Hollow the comb mellow the sweetness
Amber the honey-spoil, drink, drink.

In these windless unechoing valleys
The mind slips like a chisel-hand

Touching the surface of this clement blue
Yet must not damage the solitary Turk

Gathering his team and singing, in whose brain
The same disorder and the loneliness—

The what-we-have-in-common of us all.
Is there enough perhaps to found a world?

Then of what you said once, the passing
Of something on the road beyond the tombstones

Reflecting on dark hair with its sudden theft
Of blue from the darkness of violets

And below the nape of the neck a mole
All mixed in this odourless water-clock of hours.

So one is grateful, yes, to the ancient Greeks
For the invention of time, lustration of penitents,

Not so much for what they were
But for where we lie under the windless planes.

ON ITHACA STANDING

Tread softly, for here you stand
On miracle ground, boy.
A breath would cloud this water of glass.
Honey, bush, berry and swallow.
This rock, then, is more pastoral, than
Arcadia is, Illyria was.

Here the cold spring lilts on sand.
The temperature of the toad
Swallowing under a stone whispers: 'Diamonds.
Boy, diamonds, and juice of minerals!'
Be a saint here, dig for foxes, and water,
Mere water springs in the bones of the hands.

Turn from the hearth of the hero. Think:
Other men have their emblems, I this:
The heart's dark anvil and the crucifix
Are one, have hammered and shall hammer
A nail of flesh, me to an island cross,
Where the kestrel's arrow falls only,
The green sea licks.

EPISODE

I should set about memorising this little room,
The errors of taste which make it every other,
Like and unlike, this ugly rented bed
Now transfigured as a woman is transfigured
By love, disfigured, related and yet unrelated
To science, to the motiveless appeals of happiness.

I should set about memorising this room
It will be a long time empty and airless;
Thoughts will hang about it like mangy cats,
The mirror, vacant and idiotic as an actress
Reflect darkness, cavity of an old tooth,
A house shut up, a garden left untended.

This is probably the very moment to store it all,
Earlobes tasting of salt, a dying language
Of perfume, and the heart of someone
Hanging open on its hinges like a gate;
Rice-powder on a sleeve and two dead pillows
The telephone shook and shook but could not wake.

THE EGG

Who first wrapped love in a green leaf,
And spread warm wings on the egg of death,
That my heart was hatched like a smooth stone,
And love in a green leaf locked?

Pity was naked: who dried her feathers
By the ancient pillow with cold ankles?
(Pity, my friend, fell in with the scorpion:
Murder with his bottle took my sweet.)

Who found passion without a leg,
Shrieked like the canticle of a ghost?
A bat spat his blood in the nursery:
A vessel in darkness but without a compass.

Anger first opened the book of the egg,
A bible of broken boys and natural women.
The choir sang like a bee in a bush,
And hunger, the dog, hummed in his paws.

Now time is wrapped in a green bay-leaf,
And a Roman summer covers the underworld,
O remember the heart hatched like cold stone,
And love in a green leaf locked.

EGYPTIAN POEM

And to-day death comes to the house.
To-day upon the waters, the sunset sail,
Death enters and the swallow's eye
Under the roof is no larger and darker
Than this scent of death.

A disciple crossed over by water.
The acorn was planted.
In the Ionian villa among the marble
The fountain plays the sea's piano,
And by the clock the geometric philosopher
Walks in white linen while death
Squats in the swallow's eye.

The dogs are muzzled. Lord,
See to the outer gate, our protection.
I rest between the born and the unborn.
The father, the mother, the baby unicorn
Intercede for me, attended the christening.
Exempt me.
I have friends in the underworld.

A SMALL SCRIPTURE

Now when the angler by Bethlehem's water
Like a sad tree threw down his trance
What good was the needle of resurrection,
A bat-like soul for the father Adam,
But to bury in haystacks of common argument
The Fish's living ordinance?

A bleeding egg was the pain of testament,
Murder of self within murder to reach the Self:
The grapnel of fury like a husband's razor
Turned on his daughter in a weird enchantment
To cut out the iron mask from the iron man,
His double, the troubled elf.

Now one eye was the cyclop's monstrous ration,
But this face looked forward to Heliopolis,
Rehearsed its charm in other exilic lovers
God-bound near Eden on the crutches of guilt;
Aimed like a pistol through the yellow eyes—
Your heart and mine know the truth of this.

This we make to the double Jesus, the nonpareil,
Whose thought snapped Jordan like a dam.
Darling and bully with the bloody taws,
Both walked in this tall queen by the green lake.
Both married when the aching nail sank home.
Weep for the lion, kneel to the lamb.

EXILE IN ATHENS

To be a king of islands,
Share a boundary with eagles,
Be a subject of sails.

Here, on these white rocks,
In cold palaces all winter,
Under the salt blanket,

Forget not yet the tried intent,
Pale hands before the face: face
Before the sea's blue negative,

Washing against the night,
Pushing against the doors,
Earth's dark metaphors.

Here alone in a stone city
I sing the rock, the sea-squill,
Over Greece the one punctual star.

To be king of the clock—
I know, I know—to share
Boundaries with the bird,

With the ant her lodge:
But they betray, betray.
To be the owner of stones,

To be a king of islands,
Share a bed with a star,
Be a subject of sails.

AT EPIDAURUS

The islands which whisper to the ambitious,
Washed all winter by the surviving stars
Are here hardly recalled: or only as
Stone choirs for the sea-bird,
Stone chairs for the statues of fishermen.
This civilized valley was dedicated to
The cult of the circle, the contemplation
And correction of famous maladies
Which the repeating flesh has bred in us also
By a continuous babyhood, like the worm in meat.

The only disorder is in what we bring here:
Cars drifting like leaves over the glades,
The penetration of clocks striking in London,
The composure of dolls and fanatics,
Financed migrations to the oldest sources:
A theatre where redemption was enacted,
Repentance won, the stones heavy with dew.
The olive signs the hill, signifying revival,
And the swallow's cot in the ruin seems how
Small yet defiant an exaggeration of love!

Here we can carry our own small deaths
With the resignation of place and identity;
A temple set severely like a dice
In the vale's Vergilian shade; once apparently
Ruled from the whitest light of the summer:
A formula for marble when the clouds
Troubled the architect, and the hill spoke
Volumes of thunder, the sibyllic god wept.
Here we are safe from everything but ourselves,

The dying leaves and the reports of love.
The land's lie, held safe from the sea,
Encourages the austerity of the grass chambers,
Provides a context understandably natural
For men who could divulge the forms of gods.
Here the mathematician entered his own problem,
A house built round his identity,
Round the fond yet mysterious seasons
Of green grass, the teaching of summer-astronomy.
Here the lover made his calculations by ferns,
And the hum of the chorus enchanged.
We, like the winter, are only visitors,
To prosper here the breathing grass,

Encouraging petals on a terrace, disturbing
Nothing, enduring the sun like girls
In a town window. The earth's flower
Blows here original with every spring,
Shines in the rising of a man's age
Into cold texts and precedents for time.
Everything is a slave to the ancestor, the order
Of old captains who sleep in the hill.

Then smile, my dear, above the holy wands,
Make the indefinite gesture of the hands,
Unlocking this world which is not our world.
The somnambulists walk again in the north
With the long black rifles, to bring us answers.
Useless a morality for slaves: useless
The shouting at echoes to silence them.
Most useless inhabitants of the kind blue air,
Four ragged travellers in Homer.
All causes end within the great Because.

GREEK CHURCH: ALEXANDRIA

The evil and the good seem undistinguished,
Indeed all half asleep; their coming was
No eloquent proposition of natures
Too dense for material ends, quartered in pain.
But a propitiation by dreams of belief
A relief from the chafing ropes of thought.

Piled high in Byzane like a treasure-ship
The church heels over, sinking in sound
And yellow lamplight while the arks and trolleys
And blazing crockery of the orthodox God
Make it a fearful pomp for peasants,
A sorcery to the black-coated rational,
To the town-girl an adventure, an adventure.

Now however all hums and softly spins
Like a great top, the many-headed black
Majority merged in a single sea-shell.

Idle thoughts press in, amazing one—
How the theologians with beards of fire
Divided us upon the boiling grid of thought,
Or with dividers spun for us a fine
Conniving cobweb—traps for the soul.

Three sailors stand like brooms.
The altar has opened like a honeycomb;
An erect and flashing deacon like a despot howls.
Surely we might ourselves exhale
Our faults like rainbows on this incense?

If souls did fire the old Greek barber
Who cut my hair this morning would go flying,
Not stand, a hopeless, window-bound and awkward
Child at this sill of pomp,
Moved by a hunger money could not sate,
Smelling the miracle and softly sighing.

TO ARGOS

The roads lead southward, blue
Along a circumference of snow,
Identified now by the scholars
As a home for the cyclops, a habitation
For nymphs and ancient appearances.
Only the shepherd in his cowl
Who walks upon them really knows
The natural history in a sacred place;
Takes like a text of stone
A familiar cloud-shape or fortress,
Pointing at what is mutually seen,
His dark eyes wearing the crowsfoot.

Our idols have been betrayed
Not by the measurement of the dead ones
Who are lying under these mountains,
As under England our own fastidious
Heroes lie awake but do not judge.
Winter rubs at the ice like a hair,
Dividing time; and a single tree
Reflects here a mythical river.
Water limps on ice, or scribbles
On doors of sand its syllables,
All alone, in an empty land, alone.
This is what breaks the heart.

We say that the blood of Virgil
Grew again in the scarlet pompion,
Ever afterwards reserving the old poet
Memorials in his air, his water: so
In this land one encounters always

Agamemnon, Agamemnon; the voice
Of water falling on hair in caves,
The stonebreaker's hammer on walls,
A name held closer in the circles
Of bald granite than even these cyclamen,
Like children's ears attentive here,
Blown like glass from the floors of snow.

Truly, we the endowed who pass here
With the assurance of visitors in rugs
Can raise from the menhir no ghost
By the cold sound of English idioms.
Our true parenthood rests with the eagle,
We recognize him turning over his vaults.
Bones have no mouths to smile with
From the beds of companionable rivers dry.
The modern girls pose on a tomb smiling;
Night watches us on the western horn;
The hyssop and the vinegar have lost their meaning,
And this is what breaks the heart.

IN ARCADIA

By divination came the Dorians,
Under a punishment composed an arch.
They invented this valley, they taught
The rock to flow with odourless water.

Fire and a brute art came among them.

Rain fell, tasting of the sky.
Trees grew, composing a grammar.
The river, the river you see was brought down
By force of prayer upon this fertile floor.

Now small skills: the fingers laid upon
The nostrils of flutes, the speech of women
Whose tutors were the birds; who singing
Now civilized their children with the kiss.

Lastly, the tripod sentenced them.

Ash closed on the surviving sons.
The brown bee memorized here, rehearsed
Migration from an inherited habit.
All travellers recorded an empty zone.

Between rocks 'O death', the survivors.
O world of bushes eaten like a moon,
Kissed by the awkward patience of the ant.
Within a concave blue and void of space.

Something died out by this river: but it seems
Less than a nightingale ago.

SUMMER IN CORFU

At last the serious days of summer,
When from the red forge dancing,
The blacksmith sunshine hammers
New beaks for the flesh.
From the black mint
Steel for new flint.

State me no theme for misery. The season
Like a woman lies open, is folding,
Secret, growth upon growth. The black fig
Desire is torn again from the belly of reason.
Our summer is gravid at last, is big.

All you, who know desire in these seas,
Have souls or equipment for loneliness, loneliness,
Lean now like fruitage. The Hesperides
Open. This is the limbo, the doldrum.
Seal down the eye of your cyclops,
Silence Time's drum.

FATHER NICHOLAS HIS DEATH:
CORFU

Hush the old bones their vegetable sleep,
For the islands will never grow old.
Nor like Atlantis on a Monday tumble,
Struck like soft gongs in the amazing blue.

Dip the skull's chinks in lichens and sleep,
Old man, beside the water-gentry.
The hero standing knee-deep in his dreams
Will find and bind the name upon his atlas,
And put beside it only an X marked spot.

Leave memory to the two tall sons and lie
Calmed in smiles by the elegiac blue.
A man's address to God is the skeleton's humour,
A music sipped by the flowers.

Consider please the continuous nature of Love:
How one man dying and another smiling
Conserve for the maggot only a seed of pity,
As in winter's taciturn womb we see already
A small and woollen lamb on a hilltop hopping.

The dying and the becoming are one thing,
So wherever you go the musical always is;
Now what are your pains to the Great Danube's pains,
Your pyramids of despair against Ithaca
Or the underground rivers of Dis?

Your innocence shall be as the clear cistern
Where the lone animal in these odourless waters
Quaffs at his own reflection a shining ink.
Here at your green pasture the old psalms
Shall kneel like humble brutes and drink.

Hush then the finger bones their mineral doze
For the islands will never be old or cold
Nor ever the less blue: for the egg of beauty
Blossoms in new migrations, the whale's grey acres,
For men of the labyrinth of the dream of death.
So sleep.
All these warm when the flesh is cold.
And the blue will keep.

AT CORINTH

At Corinth one has forgiven
The recording travellers in the same past
Who first entered this land of doors,
Hunting a precise emotion by clues,
Haunting a river, or a place in a book.
Here the continuous evocations are washed
Harder than tears and brighter,
But less penetrating than the touch of flesh,
(Our fingers pressed upon eyelids of stone),
Yet more patient, surely, watching
To dissolve the statues and retire
Night after night with a dissolving moon.

The valley mist ennobles
Lovers disarmed by negligence or weather,
And before night the calm
Discovers them, breathing upon the nerves,
The scent of the exhausted lamps.
Here stars come soft to pasture,
And all doors lead to sleep.
What lies beneath the turf forbids
A footstep on the augustan stair,
The intrusion of a style less pure,
Seen through the camera's lens,
Or the quotations of visitors.

My skill is in words only:
To tell you, writing this letter home,
That we, whose blood was sweetened once
By Byron or his elders in the magic,
Entered the circle safely, found

No messenger for us except the smiles.
Owls sip the wind here. Well,
This place also was somebody's home,
Whipped by the gulf to thorns,
A house for proverbs by a broken well.
Winter was never native here: nor is.
Men, women, and the nightingales
Are forms of Spring.

THASOS

Indifferent history! In such a place
Can we choose what really matters most?
Three hundred oars munched up the gulf.
A tyrant fell. The wise men turned their beds
To face the East—this was war. Or else
Eating and excreting raised to the rank of arts:
Sporting the broad purple—this was peace,
For demagogues exhausted by sensations.
From covens of delight they brought
The silver lampreys served on deathless chargers
By cooks of polity and matchless tact.
Only their poets differed in being free
From the historic consciousness and its
Defeats: wise servants of the magnet and
The sieve, against this human backdrop told
The truth in oracles and never asked themselves
In what or why they never could believe.

ASPHODELS: CHALCIDICE

'No one will ever pick them, I think,
The ugly off-white clusters: all the grace
Lies in the name of death named.
Are they a true certificate for death?'
    'I wonder'

'You might say that once the sages,
Death being identified, forgave it language:
Called it "asphodel", as who should say
The synonym for scentless, colourless,
    Solitary,

Rock-loving . . .' 'Memory is all of these.'
'Yes, they asserted the discipline of memory,
Which admits of no relapse in its
Consignment, does not keep forever.'
    'Nor does death.'

'You mean our dying?' 'No, but when one is
Alone, neither happy nor unhappy, in
The deepest ache of reason where this love
Becomes a malefactor, clinging so,
    You surely know—'

'Death's stock will stand no panic,
Be beautiful in jars or on a coffin,
Exonerate the flesh when it has turned
Or mock the enigma with an epitaph
    It never earned.'

'These quite precisely guard ironic truth,
And you may work your way through every
Modulation of the rose, to fill your jars
With pretty writing-stuff: but for death—'
        'Truly, always give us

These comfortless, convincing, even, yes,
A little mocking, Grecian asphodels.'

IN THE GARDEN: VILLA CLEOBOLUS

The mixtures of this garden
Conduct at night the pine and oleander,
Perhaps married to dust's thin edge
Or lime where the cork-tree rubs
The quiet house, bruising the wall:

And dense the block of thrush's notes
Press like a bulb and keeping time
In this exposure to the leaves,
And as we wait the servant comes,

A candle shielded in the warm
Coarse coral of her hand, she weaves
A pathway for her in the golden leaves,
Gathers the books and ashtrays in her arm
Walking towards the lighted house,

Brings with her from the uninhabited
Frontiers of the darkness to the known
Table and tree and chair
Some half-remembered passage from a fugue
Played from some neighbour's garden
On an old horn-gramophone,

And you think: if given once
Authority over the word,
Then how to capture, praise or measure
The full round of this simple garden,
All its nonchalance at being,
How to adopt and raise its pleasure?

97

Press as on a palate this observed
And simple shape, like wine?
And from the many undeserved
Tastes of the mouth select the crude
Flavour of fruit in pottery
Coloured among this lovely neighbourhood?

Beyond, I mean, this treasure hunt
Of selves, the pains we sort to be
Confined within the loving chamber of a form,
Within a poem locked and launched
Along the hairline of the normal mind?

Perhaps not this: but somehow, yes,
To outflank the personal neurasthenia
That lies beyond in each expiring kiss:
Bring joy, as lustrous on this dish
The painted dancers motionless in play
Spin for eternity, describing for us all
The natural history of the human wish.

THE PARTHENON

Στεριὲς καὶ νησιὰ

Put it more simply: say the city
Swam up here swan-like to the shallows,
Or whiteness from an overflowing jar
Settled into this grassy violet space,
Theorem for three hills,

Went soft with brickdust, clay and whitewash,
On a plastered porch one morning wrote
Human names, think of it, men became the roads.

The academy was given over
To the investigation of shade an idle boy
Invented, tearing out the heart
Of a new loaf, put up these slender columns.

Later the Parthenon's small catafalque
Simple and congruent as a wish grew up,
Snow-blind, the marbles built upon a pause
Made smoke seem less surprising, being white.

Now syntax settled round the orderless,
Joining action and reflection in the arch,
Then adding desire and will: four walls:
Four walls, a house. 'How simple' people said.

Man entered it and woman was the roof.

99

A vexing history, Geros, that becomes
More and more simple as it ends, not less;
And nothing has redeemed it: art
Moved back from pleasure-giver to a humour

As with us . . . I see you smile . . .

Footloose on the inclining earth
The long ships moved through cities
Made of loaf-sugar, tamed by gardens,
Lying hanging by the hair within the waters

And quickened by self-knowledge
Men of linen sat on marble chairs
In self-indulgence murmuring 'I am, I am'.

Chapters of clay and whitewash. Others here
Find only a jar of red clay, a Pan
The superstitious whipped and overturned.
Yet nothing of ourselves can equal it

Though grown from causes we still share,
The natural lovely order, as where water
Touches earth, a tree grows up,
A needle touching wax, a human voice.

But for us the brush, the cone, the candle,
The spinning-wheel and clay are only
Amendments to an original joy.

Lost even the flawless finishing strokes,
White bones among the almonds prophesying
A death itself that seemed a coming-of-age.

Lastly the capes and islands hold us,
Tame as a handclasp,
Causes locked within effects, the land—
This vexed clitoris of the continental body,
Pumice and clay and whitewash
Only the darkness ever compromises

Or an eagle softly mowing on the blue . . .

And yet, Geros, who knows? Within the space
Of our own seed might some day rise,
Shriek truth, punish the blue with statues.

ETERNAL CONTEMPORARIES
SIX PORTRAITS

I

MANOLI OF COS

Down there below the temple
Where the penitents scattered
Ashes of dead birds, Manoli goes
In his leaky boat, a rose tied to the rudder.

This is not the rose of all the world,
Nor the rose of Nostradamus or of Malory:
Nor is it Eliot's clear northern rose of the mind,
But precisely and unequivocally
The red rose Manoli picked himself
From the vocabulary of roses on the hill by Cefalû.

II

MARK OF PATMOS

Mark has crossed over to Mount Olivet,
Putting aside the banneret and the drum.
He inhabits now that part of himself
Which lay formerly desolate and uncolonized.
He works that what is to pass may come
And the birth of the common heart he realized.

What passed with him? A flower dropped
In the boat by a friend, the cakes
His sister brought with the unposted letter.
Yet all the island loafers watched, disturbed,
The red sails melt into the sky, distended,
And each turned angrily to his lighted house
Feeling, not that something momentous
Had begun, but that their common childhood
Had foundered in the Syrian seas and ended.

III

BASIL THE HERMIT

Banished from the old roof-tree Patmos
Where the dynasts gathered honey,
Like dancing bears, with smoking rituals,
Or skimmed the fat of towns with levy-money,
Uncaring whether God or Paradise exist,
Laid up themselves estates in providence
While greed crouched in each hairy fist,

Basil, the troubled flower of scepticism,
Chose him a pelt, and a cairn of chilly stone,
Became the author of a famous schism:
A wick for oil, a knife, a broken stool
Were all, this side of hell, he dared to own.
For twenty years in Jesus went to school.

Often, looking up, he saw them there
As from some prism-stained pool:
Dark dots like birds along the battlements,
Old rooks swayed in a rotten tree.
They waved: he did not answer, although he
Felt kindly to them all, for they could do
What he could not: he did not dare to pray.
His inner prohibitions were a sea
On which he floated spellbound day by day.
World and its fevers howled outside: within
The Omen and the Fret that hemmed him in,
The sense of his complete unworthiness
Pressed each year slowly tighter like a tourniquet.

IV

DMITRI OF CARPATHOS

Four card-players: an ikon of the saint
On a pitted table among eight hands
That cough and spit or close like mandibles
On fortunate court-cards or on the bottle
Which on the pitted paintwork stands.
Among them one whose soft transpontine nose
Fuller of dirty pores pricked on a chart
Has stood akimbo on the turning world,
From Cimbalu to Smyrna shaken hands,
Tasted the depths of every hidden sound:
In wine or poppy a drunkard with a drunkard's heart
Who never yet was known to pay his round.

Meanwhile below in harbour his rotten boat,
Beard green from winter quarters turns
Her scraggy throat to nudge the northern star,
And like a gipsy burns and burns; goes wild
Till something climbs the hill
And stands beside him at the tavern table
To pluck his drunken elbow like a child.

V

PANAGIOTIS OF LINDOS

Dark birds in nature redevise
Their linings every year: are not
The less like these weaving fishermen
Bent so exactly at their tattered seines
On a rotten wharf, their molten catch
Now sold and loaded: though they feather only
For fathoms of sea and the fishes within it,
Needles passing in a surf of lights.

Panagiotis has resigned it all
For an enamel can and olive shade:
His concern a tavern prospect,
Miles of sweet chestnut and borage.

This armament of wine he shares now
With the greatest philosopher, the least
Inventor, the meanest doctrine of rest,
Mixing leisure and repose like wine and water,
Tutor and pupil in the crater.

His dark sleep is bruised by each
Sink of the sun below the castle
Where the Sporades have opened
Their spokes, and the whole Aegean
In brilliant soda turns the darkening bays.

VI

A RHODIAN CAPTAIN

Ten speechless knuckles lie along a knee
Among their veins, gone crooked over voyages,
Made by this ancient captain. Life has now
Contracted like the pupil of an eye
To a slit in space and time for images—

All he has seen of sage and arbutus:
Touched berries where the golden eagle crashes
From its chariot of air and dumb trap:
Islands fortunate as Atlantis was . . .
Yet while we thought him voyaging through life
He was really here, in truth, outside the doorpost,
In the shade of the eternal vine, his wife,
With the same tin plate of olives on his lap.

PENELOPE

Look, on that hill we met
On this shoreline parted.

The experts sailed off northwards
With their spears, with the connivance
Of oracles to back them. I remained.

Tears weigh little upon the hands,
Tears weigh less in the eye than seeds
Shaken from the feverish totals
Blossoming on time's pronouncing tree.

The seasons file their summaries
Overheard by the echoes in the wells,
Overlooked by the mirrors shod in horn,
Copied by spies, interpreters or witnesses.

The augurs in the delta have not *once*
Foreseen this dust upon an ageing eyeball,
Vitreous as sea-spun glass, this black
Sperm of winter sea we walk beside,
The marble onanism of these nymphs.

MATAPAN

Unrevisited perhaps forever
Southward from the capes of smoke
Where past and present to the waters are one
And the peninsula's end points out
Three fingers down the night:
On a corridor of darkness a beam
To where the islands, at last, the islands . . .

Abstract and more lovely
Andros Delos and Santorin,
Transpontine headlands in crisp weather,
Cries amputated by the gulls,
Formless, yet made in marble
Whose calm insoluble statues wear
Stone vines for hair, forever sharing
A sea-penumbra, the darkened arc
Where mythology walks in a wave
And the islands are.

Leaving you, hills, we were unaware
Or only as sleepwalkers are aware
Of a key turned in the heart, a letter
Posted under the door of an empty house;
Now Matapan and her forebodings
Became an identity, a trial of conduct,
Rolled and unrolled by the surges
Like a chart, mapped by a star,
With thistle and trefoil blowing,
An end of everything known
A beginning of water.

Here sorrow and beauty shared
Like time and place an eternal relation,
Matapan . . .

Here we learned that the lover
Is contained by love, not containing,
Matapan, Matapan:

Here the lucky in summer
Tied up their boats; a mile from land
The cicada's small machine came like a breath;
Touching bottom saw their feet become
Webbed and monstrous on the sandy floors.
Here wind emptied the snowy caves: the brown

Hands about the tiller unbuckled.
Day lay like a mirror in the sun's eye.
Olives sleeping, rocks hanging, sea shining
And under Arbutus the scriptural music
Of a pipe beside a boy beside a bay
Soliloquised in seven liquid quibbles.

Here the lucky in summer
Made fast like islanders
And saw upon the waters, leaning down
The haunted eyes in faces torn from books:
So painted the two dark-blue Aegean eyes
And θεὸς δίκαιος 'God the Just'
Under them upon the rotting prows.

Inhabitants of reflection going:
We saw the dog-rose abloom in bowls,
Faces of wishing children in the wells

Under the Acropolis the timeless urchin
Carrying the wooden swallow,
Teller of the spring; on the hills of hair
Over Athens saw the night exhaling.

Later in islands, awaiting passage,
By waters like skin and promontories,
Were blessed by the rotation
Of peach-wind, melon-wind,
Fig-wind and wind of lemons;
Every fruit in the rotation of its breath.
And in the hills encountered
Sagacious and venerable faces
Like horn spoons: forms of address:
Christian names, politeness to strangers.

> *Heard the ant's pastoral reflections:*
> *'Here I go in Arcadia, one two*
> *Saffron, sage, bergamot, rue,*
> *A root, a hair, a bead—all warm.*
> *A human finger swarming*
> *With little currents: a ring:*
> *A married man.'*

In a late winter of mist and pelicans
Saw the thread run out at last; the man
Kiss his wife and child good-bye
Under the olive-press, turning on a heel.
To enter April like swimmer,
And memory opened in him like a vein,
Pushed clear on the tides a pathless keel.

Standing alone on the hills
Saw all Greece, the human
Body of this sky suspending a world
Within a crystal turning,
Guarded by the green wicks of cypresses.

Far out on the blue
Like notes of music on a page
The two heads: the man and his wife.
They are always there.

It is too far to hear the singing.

THE ANECDOTES

I

Garcia, when you drew off those two
White bullfighting gloves your hairy
Fingers spread themselves apart,
And then contracted to a hand again,
Attached to an arm, leading to a heart,
And I suddenly saw the cottage scene
Where the knocking on the door is repeated
Nobody answers it: but inside the room
The fox has its head under the madman's shirt.

II

IN CAIRO

Nostos home: *algos* pain: nostalgia . . .

The homing pain for such as are attached:
Odours that hit and rebuff in some garden
Behind the consul's house, the shutters drawn:
In the dark street brushed by a woman's laugh.
Ursa Major to the sailor could spell wounds,
More than the mauling of the northern bear,
At the hub of the green wheel, standing on the sea.

Home for most is what you can least bear.
Ego gigno lumen, I beget light

But darkness is also of my nature.
(For such as sail out beyond
The proper limits of their own freewill.)

III

Anonymous hand, record one afternoon,
In May, some time before the fig-leaf:
Boats lying idle in the sky, a town
Thrown as on a screen of watered silk,
Lying on its side, reddish and soluble,
A sheet of glass leading down into the sea . . .

Down here an idle boy catches a cicada:
Imprisons it, laughing, in his sister's cloak
In whose warm folds the silly creature sings.

Shape of boats, body of a young girl, cicada,
Conspire and join each other here,
In twelve sad lines against the dark.

IV

AT RHODES

If space curves how much the more thought,
Returning after every conjugation
To the young point of rest it started in?

The fulness of being is not in refinement,
By the delimitation of the object, but
In roundness, the embosoming of the Real.

The egg, the cone, the rhombus: orders of reality
Which declaim coldly against the reason:
We may surround and view from every side,

We may expound, break into fields of thought,
But qualifying in this manner only spoil:
On this derogatory wheel stands Man.

Now who is greater than his greatest appetite?
Who is weaker than the least of his fears?
Who claims that he can match them perfectly,
Apprehended without to unapprehended within?

We Greeks were taught how to exhaust ideas,
Melissa, but first begin with people. There we score!
No Roman understood our sunny concupiscence,
The fast republican colour of our values.

Philosophy with us was not worked out.
We used experience up. The rest precipitated.
Soon we were still alive: but nothing else was left.

V

IN ATHENS

At last with four peroxide whores
Like doped marigolds growing upon this balcony,
We wait for sunrise, all conscripted

From our passions by the tedium and spleen,
While the rich dews are forming
On the mind of space already thick enough
To cut with scythes on the web marbles
Of Acropolis, intentions murdered by the cold,
I take her in my arms, a cobweb full of diamonds,
Which by some culture might be tears or pearls . . .

One speaks Turkish, slender as an ilex,
Half asleep is boiling an egg;
A Jewess, lovely, conspiratorial,
Over a spirit-lamp by an hour-glass
Too small to have been made for timing
Anything much longer than a kiss.

VI

AT ALEXANDRIA

Wind among prisms all tonight again:
Alone again, awake again in the Sufi's house,
Cumbered by this unexpiring love,
Jammed like a cartridge in the breech
Leaving the bed with its dented pillow,
The married shoes alert upon the floor.

Is life more than the sum of its errors?
Tubs of clear flesh, egyptian women:
Favours, kohl, nigger's taste of seeds,
Pepper or lemon, breaking from one's teeth
Bifurcated as the groaning stalks of celery.

Much later comes the tapping on the panel.
The raven in the grounds:
At four thirty the smell of satin, leather:
Rain falling in the mirror above the mad
Jumbled pots of expensive scent and fard,
And the sense of some great impending scandal.

VII

AT ALEXANDRIA

Sometime we shall all come together
And it will be time to put a stop
To this little rubbing together of minimal words,
To let the Word Prime repose in its mode
As yolk in its fort of albumen reposes,
Contented by the circular propriety
Of its hammock in the formal breathing egg.

Much as in sculpture the idea
Must not of its own anecdotal grossness
Sink through the armature of the material,
The model of its earthly clothing:
But be a plumbline to its weight in space . . .

The whole resting upon the ideogram
As on a knifeblade, never really cutting,
Yet always sharp, like this very metaphor
For perpetual and *useless* suffering exposed
By conscience in the very act of writing.

VIII

Quiet room, four candles, red wine in pottery:
Our conversation burning like a fuse,
In this cone of light like some emulsion:
Aristarchus of Samos was only half a man
Believing he could make it all coherent
Without the muddled limits of a woman's arm,
Darning a ladder, warming the begging-bowl.

Quiet force of candles burning in pools of oak,
Conducted by the annals of the word
Towards poor Aristarchus. If he was only half
A man, Melissa, then I am the other half,
Not in believing with him but by failing to.

IX

IN PATMOS

'Art adorns'. Thus Galbo.
Proconsuls should be taught to leave art alone,
Before we came the men of the east
Knew it contained a capital metaphysic,
As chess once founded in astronomy
Degenerated into the game we know.

For the Western man of this Egopetal Age
Cant, rules, pains and prohibitions,
Each with its violent repulsive force.

117

Only in this still round, touching hands,
To live and lapse and die created,
As Socrates died penniless to leave a fortune.

X

When they brought on the sleeping child
Bandaged on its glittering trolley
One could think no more of anecdotes:
Ugly Sappho lying under an acorn wishing,
Cyrano discountenanced by a nose like a wen,
My father's shadow telling me three times
Not to play with the scissors: None of this,
But of something inanimate about to be cut up:
A loaf with the oven scent on it exhaling
A breath of sacrifice, clouding the knife.

XI

IN BRITAIN

Instead of this or that fictitious woman
Marry a cloud and carve it in a likeness.

XII

IN RHODES

Incision of a comb in hair: lips stained
Blue as glass windows with the grapes
We picked and tasted by ourselves in Greece.

Such was the yesterday that made us
Appropriates of a place, club-members
Of an oleander-grove asleep in chairs.

XIII

In youth the decimal days for spending:
Now in age they fall in heaps about me
Thick in concussion as the apples
Bouncing on drums to multiply the seasons
On the floors of scented granaries,
In memory, old barn, wrapped up in straw.

Literarum oblivio . . . Now the Romans
Are going to get the chance they ask for,
That hated jurist's tongue . . .
Their violence will be greater than ours.

Happily we shall not live to see it,
Melissa, nurse, augur, special self.
Once the statues lined the whole main-street
Like nightmares, returning from her house,
Night after night by rosy link-light,
A rose between my teeth, by any other name.

Now we sit in linen deck-chairs here
Looking out to sea and eating olives
From a painted jar: Flavia did this for me,
Won me these favours, this exile from myself.
The exile I had already begun, within myself
She translated like a linguist: Paris.

The King was a bore: it was not my fault he was:
I loved her because I did not know myself.
I knew her yet in the shadow cast by myself
My love was hidden. How we deceive ourselves!
Only our friends know if our wives are faithful,
They will never tell us. (Marc smiling.)

Anyway, now, this animal concupiscence
Of old age in a treaty port: still only consul.
The meteors and the wild mares
Are growing manes, my dear. Autumn is on the way.

We crouch in the wrecked shooting-galleries of
    progress . . .

And where you turn, black head of grapes, the sea
Is bluer than forget-me-nots are blue,
Where the linguist in you paraphrases sadly:
The heart must be very old to feel so young.

XIV

IN BEIRUT

After twenty years another meeting,
Those faces round, as circumspect as eggshells:
But in the candle-light fard
Depicts its own origins and ends:
Flesh murky as old horn,
Hands dry now as sea-biscuit,
Sipping the terrible beat of Time

We talk about the past as if it were not
Dead, that April when the ships pouted
From breathless harbours north of Tenedos,
And the green blood of the Delphic bushes
Put back their ears
Where the Greek wind ran, insisted, and became.

Then of poor Clea: her soul sickened in her face
Like flowers in some shadowy sick-room,
How to recall that wingless sickle of a nose,
Thinned out and famished into fever:
The liquid drops of eyes, darkened by carbon,
Brusque ways, an imperative style and voice—
Always catching her dress in doors . . .

Can we afford to consider ourselves more fortunate?
Lips I would have died to hear speak
Now held in complete sesame here
By a fire of blue sea-coal,
In Tunis, winter coming on.

XV

IN RHODES

From the intellect's grosser denominations
I can sort one or two, how indistinctly,
Living on as if in some unripened faculty
Quite willing to release them, let them die.

Putative mothers-in-ideas like that Electra's
Tallow orphan skin in a bed smelling faintly
Of camphor, the world, the harsh laugh of Glauca:

But both like geometrical figures now,
Then musky, carmine . . . (I am hunting for
The precise shade of pink for Acte's mouth:
Pink as the sex of a mastiff . . .)

Now as the great paunch of this earth
Allows its punctuation by seeds, some to be
Trees, some men walking as trees, so the mind
Offers its cakes of spore to time in them:
The sumptuary pleasure-givers living on
In qualities as sure as taste of hair and mouth,
White partings of the hair like highways,
Permutations of a rose, buried beneath us now,
Under the skin of thinking like a gland
Discharging its obligations in something trivial:
Say a kiss, a handclasp: say a stone tear.

They went. We did not hear them leave.
They came. We were not ready for them.
Then turning the sphere to death
Which like some great banking corporation
Threatens, forecloses, and from all
Our poses selects the one sea-change—
Naturally one must smile to see him powerless
Not in the face of these small fictions
But in the greater one they nourished
By exhaustion of the surfaces of life,
Leaving the True Way, so that suddenly
We no longer haunted the streets
Of our native city, guilty as a popular singer,
Clad in the fur of some wild animal.

XVI

IN RIO

And so at last goodbye,
For time does not heed its own expenditure,
As the heart does in making old,
Infecting memory with a sigh-by-sigh,
Or the intolerable suppurating hope and wish.

It has no copy, moves in its own
Blind illumination seriously,
Traced somewhere perhaps by a yellow philosopher
Motionless over a swanpan,
Who found the door open—it always is:
Who found the fire banked: it never goes out.

We, my dear Melissa, are only typics of
This Graeco-Roman asylum, dedicated here
To an age of Bogue, where the will sticks
Like a thorn under the tongue,
Making our accent pain and not completeness.

Do not interrupt me . . . Let me finish:
Madmen established in the intellect
By the domestic error of a mind that arranges,
Explains, but can never sufficiently include:
Punishes, exclaims, but never completes its arc
To enter the Round. Nor all the cabals
Of pity and endurance in the circus of art
Will change it till the mainspring will is broken.

Yet the thing can be done, as you say, simply
By sitting and waiting, the mystical leap
Is only a figure for it, it involves not daring
But the patience, being gored, not to cry out.
But perhaps even the desire itself is dying.
I should like that: to make an end of it.

It is time we did away with this kind of suffering,
It has become a pose and refuge for the lazy:
As for me I must do as I was born
And so must you: upon the smaller part of the circle
We desire fulfilment in the measure of our gift:

You kiss and make: while I withdraw and plead.

CONON IN EXILE

I

Three women have slept with my books,
Penelope among admirers of the ballads,
Let down her hair over my exercises
But was hardly aware of me; an author
Of tunes which made men like performing dogs;
She did not die but left me for a singer in a wig.

II

Later Ariadne read of *The Universe*,
Made a journey under the islands from her own
Green home, husband, house with olive trees.
She lay with my words and let me breathe
Upon her face; later fell like a gull from the
Great ledge in Scio. Relations touched her body
Warm and rosy from the oil like a scented loaf,
Not human any more—but not divine as they had hoped.

III

You who pass the islands will perhaps remember
The lovely Ion, harmless, patient and in love.
Our quarrels disturbed the swallows in the eaves,
The wild bees could not work in the vine;

Shaken and ill, one of true love's experiments,
It was she who lay in the stone bath dry-eyed,
Having the impression that her body had become
A huge tear about to drop from the eye of the world.
We never learned that marriage is a kind of architecture,
The nursery virtues were missing, all of them,
So nobody could tell us why we suffered.

IV

It would be untrue to say that *The Art of Marriage*
And the others: *Of Peace in the Self* and *Of Love*
Brought me no women; I remember bodies, arms, faces,
But I have forgotten their names.

V

Finally I am here. Conon in exile on Andros
Like a spider in a bottle writing the immortal
Of Love and Death, through the bodies of those
Who slept with my words but did not know me.
An old man with a skinful of wine
Living from pillow to poke under a vine.

At night the sea roars under the cliffs.
The past harms no one who lies close to the Gods.
Even in these notes upon myself I see
I have put down women's names like some
Philosophical proposition. At last I understand

They were only forms for my own ideas,
With names and mouths and different voices.
In them I lay with myself, my style of life,
Knowing only coitus with the shadows,
By our blue Aegean which forever
Washes and pardons and brings us home.

BY THE LAKE

If seen by many minds at once your image
As in a prism falling breaks itself,
Or looking upwards from a gleaming spoon
Defies: a smile squeezed up and vanishing
In roundels of diversion like the moon.

Yet here you are confirmed by the smallest
Wish or kiss upon the rising darkness
But rootless as a wick afloat in water,
Fatherless as shoes walking over dead leaves;
A patient whom no envy stirs but joy
And what the harsh chords of experience leaves—

This dark soft eye, so liquid now and hoarse
With pleasure: or your arms in mirrors
Combing out softly hair
As lovely as a planet's and remote.

How many several small forevers
Whispered in the rind of the ear
Melissa, by this Mediterranean sea-edge,
Captured and told?
How many additions to the total silence?

Surely we increased you by very little,
But as with a net or gun to make your victims men?

THE NIGHT

Cut from the joints of this immense
Darkness upon the face of Egypt lying,
We move in the possession of our acts
Alone, the dread apostles of our weakness.

For look. The mauve street is swallowed
And the bats have begun to stitch slowly.
At the stable-door the carpenter's three sons
Bend over a bucket of burning shavings,
Warming their inwardness and quite unearthly
As the candle-marking time begins.

Three little magi under vast Capella,
Beloved of all as shy as the astronomer,
She troubles heaven with her golden tears,
Tears flowing down upon us at this window,
The children rapt, the mauve street swallowed,
The harps of flame among the shadows
In Egypt now and far from Nazareth.

THE ADEPTS

Some, the great Adepts, found it
A lesser part of them—ashes and thorns—
Where this sea-sickness on a bed
Proved nothing calm and virginal,
But animal, unstable, heavy as lead.

Some wearied for a sex
Like a science of known relations:
A God proved through the flesh—or else a mother.
They dipped in this huge pond and found it
An ocean of shipwrecked mariners instead,
Cried out and foundered, losing one another.

But some sailed into this haven
Laughing, and completely undecided,
Expecting nothing more
Than the mad friendship of bodies,
And farewells undisguised by pride:

They wrote those poems—the diminutives of madness
While at a window someone stood and cried.

THE ENCOUNTER

At this the last yet second meeting,
Almost the autumn was postponed for us—
Season when the fermenting lovers lie
Among the gathered bunches quietly.

So formal was it, so incurious:
The chime of glasses, the explorer,
The soldier and the secret agent
With a smile inviting like a target.

Six of a summer evening, you remember.
The painful rehearsal of the smile
And the words: 'I am going into a decline,
Promised by summer but by winter disappointed.'

The face was turned as sadly as a hare's,
Provoked by prudence and discretion to repeat:
'Some of them die, you know, or go away.
Our denials are only gestures—can we help it?'

Turn to another aspect of the thing.
The cool muslin dress shaken with flowers—
It was not the thought that was unworthy
Knowing all you knew, it was the feeling.

Idly turning from the offered tea I saw
As swimmers see their past, in the lamplight
Burning, particular, fastidious and lost

Your figure forever in the same place,
Same town and country, sorting letters
On a green table from many foreign cities,
The long hare's features, the remarkable sad face.

PETRON, THE DESERT FATHER

Waterbirds sailing upon the darkness
Of Mareotis, this was the beginning:
Dry reeds touched by the shallow beaks he heard
On the sand trash of an estuary near Libya,
This dense yellow lake, ringing now
With the insupportable accents of the Word.

Common among the commoners of promise
He illustrated to the ordinary those
Who found no meaning in the flesh's weakness—
The elegant psychotics on their couches
In Alexandria, hardly tempted him,
With talks of business, war and lovely clothes.

The lemon-skinned, the gold, the half-aware
Were counters for equations he examined,
Grave as their statues fashioned from the life;
A pioneer in pleasure on the long
Linen-shaded colonnades he often heard
Girls' lips puff in the nostrils of the fife.

Now dense as clouded urine moved the lake
Whose waters were to be his ark and fort
By the harsh creed of water-fowl and snake,
To the wave-polished stone he laid his ear
And said: 'I dare not ask for what I hope,
And yet I may not speak of what I fear.'

VISITATIONS

Left like an unknown's breath on mirrors,
The enchanters, the persuaders
Whom the seasons swallow up,
Only leave us ash in saucers,
Or to mice the last invaders
Open cupboard-doors or else
Lipstick-marks upon a cup.

Fingerprint the crook of time,
Ask him what he means by it,
Eyes and thoughts and lovely bodies,
David's singing, Daphne's wit
Like Eve's apple undigested
Rot within us bit by bit.

Experience in a humour ends,
Wrapped in its own dark metaphor,
And divining winter breaks:
Now one by one the Hungers creep
Up from the orchards of the mind
Here to trouble and confuse
Old men's after-dinner sleep.

FUNCHAL

At Funchal the blackish yeast
Of the winter sea I hated rubbed
And gobbled on a thousand capes,
That crumble with the traveller's confidence
In being alone, some who still tread
Decks as if they were green lawns;
But the water coiled backwards
Like a spring to press its tides
Idle and uniform as grapes in presses
Descrying a horizontal mood,
The weather slowing like a pedal,
Smelling of sick and spices,
Red leather and the spermy polish
Men in boots rub boldly on to brass.
But night is always night even here,
Beyond the introspective glare
Of the green islands on the awnings,
St. Vincent copied in the pupils,
Marrow of romance and old sea-fevers,
Seen from a sanded rail above the sharks
On this half-deck polished like a nape.

A WATER-COLOUR OF VENICE

Zarian was saying: Florence is youth,
And after it Ravenna, age,
Then Venice, second-childhood.

The pools of burning stone where time
And water, the old siege-masters,
Have run their saps beneath
A thousand saddle-bridges,
Puffed up by marble griffins drinking,

And all set free to float on loops
Of her canals like great intestines
Now snapped off like a berg to float,
Where now, like others, you have come alone,
To trap your sunset in a yellow glass,
And watch the silversmith at work
Chasing the famous salver of the bay . . .

Here sense dissolves, combines to print only
These bitten choirs of stone on water,
To the rumble of old cloth bells,
The cadging of confetti pigeons,
A boatman singing from his long black coffin . . .

To all that has been said before
You can add nothing, only that here,
Thick as a brushstroke sleep has laid
Its fleecy unconcern on every visage,

At the bottom of every soul a spoonful of sleep.

CONON IN ALEXANDRIA

I

Ash-heap of four cultures,
Bounded by Mareotis, a salt lake,
On which the winter rain rings and whitens,
In the waters, stiffens like eyes.

I have been four years bound here:
A time for sentences by the tripod:
Prophecies by those who were born dead,
Or who lost their character but kept their taste.

A solitary presumed quite happy,
Writing those interminable whining letters,
On the long beaches dimpled by the rain,
Tasting the island wind

Blown against wet lips and shutters out of Rhodes.
I say 'presumed', but would not have it otherwise.

*   *   *

Steps go down to the port
Beyond the Pharos. O my friends,
Surely these nightly visitations
Of islands in one's sleep must soon be over?

I have watched beside the others,
But always the more attentive, the more exacting:
The familiar papers on a table by the bed,
The plate of olives and the glass of wine.

137

You would think that thoughts so long rehearsed
Like the dry friction of ropes in the mind
Would cease to lead me where in Greece
The almond-candles and the statues burn.

The moon's cold seething fires over this white city,
Through four Februaries have not forgotten.

*　　*　　*

Tonight the stars press idly on the nerves
As in a cobweb, heavy with dispersal:
Points of dew in a universe too large
Too formal to be more than terrible.

'There are sides of the self
One can seldom show. They live on and on
In an emergency of anguish always,
Waiting for parents in another.'

Would you say that later, reading
Such simple propositions, the historian
Might be found to say: 'The critic
In him made a humour of this passion.

The equations of a mind too conscious of ideas,
Fictions, not kisses, crossed the water between them'?

II

And later, Spring, which compels these separations
Will but define you further as she dies
In flowers downless and pure as Portia's cheek,
Interrupting perhaps the conversations of friends

On terraces where the fountains plane at time,
To leave this small acid precipitate to memory,
Of something small, screwed-up, and thrown aside.
'*Partings like these are lucky. At least they wound.*'

And later by the hearthstone of a philosophy
You might have added: 'The desert, yes, for exiles.
But its immensity only confines one further.
Its end seems always in oneself.'

A gown stained at the arm-pits by a woman's body.
A letter unfinished because the ink gave out.

*   *   *

The lovers you describe as '*separating each other*
Further with every kiss': and your portrait
Of a man '*engaged in bitterly waiting*
For the day when art should become unnecessary',

Were in the style and order, as when you say
'*Freedom alone confines*'; but do they show a love,
Fragmented everywhere by conscience and deceit,
Ending on this coast of torn-out lighthouses?

Or that neglected and unmerited Habit,
The structure that so long informed our growth?
Questions for a nursery wall! But are they true to these?

I have passed all this day in what they would call patience.
Not writing, alone in my window, with my flute,
Having read in a letter that last immortal February
That '*Music is only love, looking for words*'.

HIGH SIERRA

The grass they cropped converting into speed
Made green the concert of their hooves
Over the long serene sierras turning
In the axle of the sun's eye
To legs as delicate as spiders', picking out
Pathways for shadows mounted on them:
Enigma, Fosforos, and Indigo, which rumbled
Through the pursuing quarries like a wind
To where the paths fall, and we all of us
Go down with the sun, sierra by sierra, held
A moment rising in the stirrups, then abandoned
To where the black valleys from their shoes
Subtract sparks upon flints, and the long
Quivering swish of tails on flesh
Try to say 'sleep', try to say 'food' and 'home'.

SARAJEVO

Bosnia. November. And the mountain roads
Earthbound but matching perfectly these long
And passionate self-communings counter-march,
Balanced on scarps of trap, ramble or blunder
Over traverses of cloud: and here they move,
Mule-teams like insects harnessed by a bell
Upon the leaf-edge of a winter sky,

And down at last into this lap of stone
Between four cataracts of rock: a town
Peopled by sleepy eagles, whispering only
Of the sunburnt herdsman's hopeless ploy:
A sterile earth quickened by shards of rock
Where nothing grows, not even in his sleep,

Where minarets have twisted up like sugar
And a river, curdled with blond ice, drives on
Tinkling among the mule-teams and the mountaineers,
Under the bridges and the wooden trellises
Which tame the air and promise us a peace
Harmless with nightingales. None are singing now.

No history much? Perhaps. Only this ominous
Dark beauty flowering under veils,
Trapped in the spectrum of a dying style:
A village like an instinct left to rust,
Composed around the echo of a pistol-shot.

THE HIVE OF INNOCENCE

SAPPHO

Shut up from pleasure in a holy fountain,
A nymph lies, hearing the woollen water,
Softly on the cone of the ear uncurling.

CHORUS

A water-nymph, idle as innocence professed,
Woven in the hum of the hairy hive.

SAPPHO

She longs, she longs, but no one calls to her.
In lapidary totals go the water-woken syllables.
She is to love a stranger, demobilized by pleasure.

CHORUS

A water-nymph, idle as innocence professed,
Woven in the hum of the hairy hive.

SAPPHO

Who will come, one to hush the water,
Two to crush the stone, three to cherish her,
Four to fold, and five to usher her
Blushing into the world?

CHORUS

A water-nymph, washed in the commotion
Of a stony fountain-floor, O speak to her,

Speak to her within the rock.
For who can measure peace of mind,
Or halve the world of pleasure
For all the water living in the clock?

[*from 'Sappho', a play*]

MIDNIGHT DIALOGUE

SAPPHO

Beyond the capes and headlands of the wish,
Beyond the menhirs of desire premeditated,
Most awkward and timid with those who most require
One subtle and beautiful and quite at ease,
We move and founder on tides of illusion,
Fumbling outside immortality's immobile doors.

PHAON

Lucky the founders of the buried city,
Transparent their acts, their wishes and laws,
Undivided as we have been divided.

SAPPHO

Entangled in ever more meaningless wars:
Too simple, too complex, too deep, too many-sided,
We join our bones to theirs in the sea's sepulchres
To litter the bitter ocean's fluctuating floors.

PHAON

Pointless, objectless, without the grace to stamp
On history more than the impress of a typical error,
Like a hare-lip or a blue eye, handed on and on.

SAPPHO

Down the long slipways of perpetual terror,
Moved between indolence, indulgence and unknowing,
The purposeless coming and the purposeless going:
Snapped in the manacles of reviving error.

Damned in effect and still neglecting cause,
Soft brief and awkward as the kisses which combine
To intersect with death till time follows us, time
Finds and detains us here in time,
In this eternal pause,
Fumbling outside immortality's immobile doors.

[*from* 'Sappho', *a play*]

FREEDOM

O Freedom which to every man entire
Presents imagined longings to his fire,
To swans the water, bees the honey-cell,
To bats the dark, to lovers loving well,
Only to the wise may you
Restricting and confining be,
All who half-delivered from themselves
Suffer your conspiracy,
Freedom, Freedom, prison of the free.

[*from 'Sappho', a play*]

ETHIOPIA

SOLO VOICE

O fishermen, far beyond the waters,
We hear of you living in those places.

CHORUS

Beyond stone urns and statues' wooden faces
Ethiopia, in Ethiopia.

SOLO VOICE

Temples and images to Gods
Unknown by men, as yet unapprehended.

CHORUS

Voyages begun, begun but never ended
Ethiopia, in Ethiopia.

SOLO VOICE

Clouds, islands, and bereaved women
Remember you wherever the axe flashes.

CHORUS

In the falling of a million eyelashes,
Ethiopia, the many in the one,
While the midges dance on the rivers
In the eye of the sun, in the eye of the sun.

[from 'Sappho', a play]

FANGBRAND

A BIOGRAPHY

Fangbrand was here once,
A missionary man,
Borne down by the Oxus,
Pursued by the lilies,
Inhabited by the old voice of sorrows,
In a black hat and sanitary boots.

The island recognised him,
Giving no welcome, lying
Trembling among her craters:
The blue circlets of stone,
On a sea blotted with fictions.
He came to the wharf with long oars.

The Ocean's peculiar spelling
Haunts here, cuddled by syllables
In caves perpendicular, a blue recitation
Of water washing the dead,
On the pediments of the statues,
Came the strange man, the solitary man,

Fangbrand the unsuspecting,
Missionary one in thick soles,
Measuring penance by the pipkin,
Step-brother to the gannet,
Travelling the blue bowl of the world,
His virtues in him rough as towels.

His brows that bent like forests
Over the crystal-gazing eyes;
His brows that bent like forests,
A silver hair played on his neck.
He saw this rock and the seal asleep,
With the same mineral stare.

This place he made pastance
For the platonic ass; in this
Cottage by the water supported
The duellers, the twins,
Of argument and confusion,
Alone in a melancholy hat.

Those who come to this pass,
Ask themselves always how
A rock can become a parish,
Pulpits whitened by the sea-birds,
Mean more than just house, rock,
A tree, a table and a chair.

His window was Orion;
At night standing upon the deep,
His eyes smaller than commas
Watched without regret the ships
Passing, one light in a void,
One pure point on the wave's floor.

Measured in the heart's small flask
The spirit's disturbance: the one voice
Saying 'Renounce', the other
Answering 'Be'; the division
Of the darkness into faces
Crying 'Too late' 'Too late'.

At night the immediate
Rubbing of the ocean on stones,
The headlands dim in her smoke
And always the awareness
Of self like a point, the quiver
As of a foetal heart asleep in him.

Continuous memory, continual evocations.
An old man in a colony of stones,
Frowning, exilic, upon a thorn,
Learning nothing of time:
Sometimes in a windy night asleep
His lips brushed the forbidden apples.

Everything reproached him, the cypress
Revising her reflection in pools,
The olive's stubborn silver in wind,
The nude and statuary hills all
Saying 'Turn back. Turn back.
Peace lies another way, old man'.

It seemed to him here at last
His age, his time, his sex even
Were struck and past; life
In a flood carrying all idols
Into the darkness, struck
Like floating tubs, and were gone.

The pathfinder rested now,
The sick man found silence
Like the curved ear of a shell;
A roar of silence even
Diminishing the foolish cool
Haunting note of the dove.

By day he broke his fruit
Humbly from the tree: his water
From wells as deep as Truth:
Living on snails and waterberries,
Marvelling for the first time
At the luminous island, the light.

His body he left in pools
Now dazed by fortune, like an old
White cloth discarded where
Only the fish were visitors.
Their soft perverted kisses
Melted the water on his side.

The rich shadow of the vine's tent
Like a cold cloth on his skull;
Spring water blown through sand,
Bubbled on mineral floors,
Ripened in smooth cisterns
Dripped from a hairy lintel on his tongue.

Truth's metaphor is the needle,
The magnetic north of purpose
Striving against the true north
Of self: Fangbrand found it out,
The final dualism in very self,
An old man holding an asphodel.

Everywhere night lay spilled,
Like coolness from spoons,
And his to drink, the human
Surface of the sky, the planes
And concaves of the eye reflecting
A travelling mirror, the earth.

He regarded himself in water,
The torrid brow's beetle,
The grammarian's cranium-bone.
He regarded himself in water
Saying 'X marks the spot,
Self, you are still alive!'

From now the famous ten-year
Silence fell on him; disciples
Invented the legend; now
They search the white island
For a book perhaps, a small
Paper of revelation left behind.

Comb out the populous waters,
Study the mud: what kept,
Held, fed, fattened him?
The hefts of stone are the only
Blossoms here: nothing grows,
But the ocean expunges.

Time's chemicals mock the hunter
For crumbs of doctrine; Fangbrand
Died with his art like a vase.
The grave in the rock,
Sweetened by saffron, bubbles water
Like a smile, an animal truth.

Death interrupted nothing.
Like guarded towns against alarms,
Our sentries in the nerves
Never sleep; but his one night
Slept on their arms, Hesperus shining,
And the unknowns entered.

So the riders of the darkness pass
On their circuit: the luminous island
Of the self trembles and waits,
Waits for us all, my friends,
Where the sea's big brush recolours
The dying lives, and the unborn smiles.

Mykonos

JOHN DONNE

From the dark viands of the church
His food in tortured verse he wore
Impersonating with each kiss
All that he feared of love and more,

For each must earn his thorny crown
And each his poisoned kiss,
Whoever quarries pain will find
By that remove or this

The sacrament the lovers took
In wine-dark verse suborned his book,

In every sensual measure heard
The chuckles of the daemon Word.
He saw the dark blood in the cup
Which one day drank his being up.

A PORTRAIT OF THEODORA

I recall her by a freckle of gold
In the pupil of one eye, an odd
Strawberry-gold: and after many years
Of forgetting that musical body—
Arms too long, wrists too slender—
Remember only the unstable wishes
Disquieting the flesh. I will not
Deny her pomp was laughable, urban:
Behind it one could hear the sad
Provincial laughter rotted by insomnia.

None of these meetings are planned,
I guess, or willed by the exemplars
Of a city's love—a city founded in
The name of love: to me is always
Brown face, white teeth, cheap summer frock
In green and white stripes and then
Forever a strawberry eye. I recalled no more
For years. The eye was lying in wait.

Then in another city from the same
Twice-used air and sheets, in the midst
Of a parting: the same dark bedroom,
Arctic chamber-pot and cruel iron bed,
I saw the street-lamp unpick Theodora
Like an old sweater, unwrinkle eyes and mouth,
Unbandaging her youth to let me see
The wounds I had not understood before.

How could I have ignored such wounds?
The bloody sweepings of a loving smile
Strewed like Osiris among the dunes?
Now only my experience recognizes her
Too late, among the other great survivors
Of the city's rage, and places her among
The champions of love—among the true elect!

CAVAFY

I like to see so much the old man's loves
Egregious if you like and often shabby
Protruding from the ass's skin of verse,
For better or for worse,
The bones of poems cultured by a thirst—
Dilapidated taverns, dark eyes washed
Now in the wry and loving brilliance
Of such barbaric memories
As held them when the dyes of passion ran.
No cant about the sottishness of man!

The forest of dark eyes he mused upon,
Out of ikons, waking beside his own
In stuffy brothels on stained mattresses,
Watched by the melting vision of the flesh,
Eros the tutor of our callowness
Deployed like ants across his ageing flesh
The crises of great art, the riders
Of love, their bloody lariats whistling,
The cries locked in the quickened breath,
The love-feast of a sort of love-in-death.

And here I find him great. Never
To attempt a masterpiece of size—
You must leave life for that. No
But always to preserve the adventive
Minute, never to destroy the truth
Admit the coarse manipulations of the lie.
If only the brown fingers franking his love
Could once be fixed in art, the immortal
Episode be recorded—*there* he would awake

On a fine day to shed his acts like scabs,
The trespasses on life and living slake

In the taste, not of his death but of his dying:
And like the rest of us he died still trying.

BYRON

The trees have been rapping
At these empty casements for a year,
Have been rapping and tapping and
Repeating to us here
Omens of the defeating wind,
Omens of the defeating mind.

Headquarters of a war
House in a fever-swamp
Headquarters of a mind at odds.

Before me now lies Byron and behind,
Belonging to the Gods,
Another Byron of the feeling
Shown in this barbered hairless man,
Splashed by the candle-stems
In his expensive cloak and wig
And boots upon the dirty ceiling.

Hobbled by this shadow,
My own invention of myself, I go
In wind, rain, stars, climbing
This ladder of compromises into Greece
Which like the Notself looms before
My politics, my invention and my war.
None of it but belongs
To this farded character
Whose Grecian credits are his old excuse
By freedom holding Byron in abuse.

Strange for one who was happier
Tuned to women, to seek and sift
In the heart's simple mesh,
To know so certainly
Under the perfume and the politics
What undertow of odours haunts the flesh:
Could once resume them all
In lines that gave me rest,
And watch the fat fly Death
Hunting the skeleton down in each,
Like hairs in plaster growing,
Promising under the living red the yellow—
I helped these pretty children by their sex
Discountenance the horrid fellow.

I have been a secretary (I sing)
A secretary to love . . .

In this bad opera landscape
Trees, fevers and quarrels
Spread like sores: while the gilded
Abstractions like our pride and honour
On this brute age close like doors
Which pushing does not budge.

Outside them, I speak for the great average.
My disobedience became
A disguise for a style in a new dress.
Item: a lock of hair.
Item: a miniature, myself aged three,
The innocent and the deformed
Pinned up in ribbons for posterity.

And now here comes
The famous disposition to weep,
To renounce. Picture to yourself
A lord who encircled his life
With women's arms; or another
Who rode through the wide world howling
And searching for his mother.

Picture to yourself a third: a cynic.
This weeping published rock—
The biscuits and the glass of soda-water:
Under Sunium's white cliffs
Where I laboured with my knife
To cut a 'Byron' there—
I was thinking softly of my daughter.

A cock to Aesculapius no less . . .

You will suggest we found only
In idleness and indignation here,
Plucked by the offshore dancers, brigs
Like girls, and ports of call
In our commerce with liberty, the Whore,
Through these unbarbered priests
And garlic-eating captains:
Fame like the only porch in a wall
To squeeze our shelter from
By profit and by circumstance
Assist this rocky nation's funeral.

The humane and the lawful in whom
Art and manners mix, who sent us here,
This sort of figures from a drawing-room

Should be paused themselves once
Under these legendary islands.
A landscape hurled into the air
And fallen on itself: we should see
Where the frail spines of rivers
Soft on the backbone intersect and scribble
These unbarbered gangs of freedom dribble
Like music down a page and come
Into the valleys with their small
Ordnance which barks and jumps.
I, Byron: the soft head of my heart bumps
Inside me as on a vellum drum.

Other enemies intervene here,
Not less where the valet serves
In a muddle of papers and consequences;
Not less in places where I walk alone
With Conscience, the defective: my defences
Against a past which lies behind,
Writing and rewriting to the bone
Those famous letters in my mind.

Time grows short. Now the trees
Are rapping at the empty casements.
Fevers are closing in on us at last—
So long desired an end of service
To the flesh and its competitions of endurance.
There is so little time. Fletcher
Tidies the bed at dusk and brings me coffee.

You, the speaking and the feeling who come after:
I sent you something once—it must be
Somewhere in *Juan*—it has not reached you yet.

O watch for this remote
But very self of Byron and of me,
Blown empty on the white cliffs of the mind,
A dispossessed His Lordship writing you
A message in a bottle dropped at sea.

LA ROCHEFOUCAULD

'Nous arrivons tout nouveaux aux divers âges
de la vie'

'A penny for your thoughts. I wasn't joking.'
Most of it I learned from serving-girls,
Looking into eyes mindless as birds, taking
The pure for subject or the unaware.
When empty mouths so soon betray their fear
Kisses can be probes. Mine always were.

Yes, everywhere I sorted the betraying
Motive, point by point designed
This first detective-story of the heart,
Judge, jury, victim, all were in my aspect,
Pinned on the clear notation of the mind—
I primed them like an actor in a part.

I was my own motive—I see you smile:
The one part of me I *never* used or wrote,
Every comma paused there, hungry
To confess me, to reveal the famished note.

Yet in reason I mastered appetite,
And taught myself at last the tragic sense;
Then through appetite and its many ambushes
I uncovered the politics of feeling, dense
Groves for the flocks of sin to feed in.
Yet in the end the portrait always seemed
Somehow faked, or somehow still in need
Of gender, form and present tense.

I could not get beyond this wall.

No. The bait of feeling was left untasted:
Deep inside like ruins lay the desires
To give, to trust, to be my subjects' equal,
All wasted, wasted.
Though love is not the word I want
Yet it will have to do. There is no other.

So the great Lack grew and grew.
Of the Real Darkness not one grain I lifted.
Yet the whole story is here like the part
Of some great man's body,
Veins, organs, nerves,
Unhappily illustrating neither death nor art.

ON FIRST LOOKING INTO
LOEB'S HORACE

I found your Horace with the writing in it;
Out of time and context came upon
This lover of vines and slave to quietness,
Walking like a figure of smoke here, musing
Among his high and lovely Tuscan pines.

All the small-holder's ambitions, the yield
Of wine-bearing grape, pruning and drainage
Laid out by laws, almost like the austere
Shell of his verses—a pattern of Latin thrift;
Waiting so patiently in a library for
Autumn and the drying of the apples;
The betraying hour-glass and its deathward drift.

Surely the hard blue winterset
Must have conveyed a message to him—
The premonitions that the garden heard
Shrunk in its shirt of hair beneath the stars,
How rude and feeble a tenant was the self,
An Empire, the body with its members dying—
And unwhistling now the vanished Roman bird?

The fruit-trees dropping apples; he counted them;
The soft bounding fruit on leafy terraces,
And turned to the consoling winter rooms
Where, facing south, began the great prayer,
With his reed laid upon the margins
Of the dead, his stainless authors,
Upright, severe on an uncomfortable chair.

Here, where your clear hand marked up
'The hated cypress' I added 'Because it grew
On tombs, revealed his fear of autumn and the urns',
Depicting a solitary at an upper window
Revising metaphors for the winter sea: 'O
Dark head of storm-tossed curls'; or silently
Watching the North Star which like a fever burns

Away the envy and neglect of the common,
Shining on this terrace, lifting up in recreation
The sad heart of Horace who must have seen it only
As a metaphor for the self and its perfection—
A burning heart quite constant in its station.

Easy to be patient in the summer,
The light running like fishes among the leaves,
Easy in August with its cones of blue
Sky uninvaded from the north; but winter
With its bareness pared his words to points
Like stars, leaving them pure but very few.

He will not know how we discerned him, disregarding
The pose of sufficiency, the landed man,
Found a suffering limb on the great Latin tree
Whose roots live in the barbarian grammar we
Use, yet based in him, his mason's tongue;
Describing clearly a bachelor, sedentary,
With a fond weakness for bronze-age conversation,
Disguising a sense of failure in a hatred for the young,

Who built in the Sabine hills this forgery
Of completeness, an orchard with a view of Rome;
Who studiously developed his sense of death

Till it was all around him, walking at the circus,
At the baths, playing dominoes in a shop—
The escape from self-knowledge with its tragic
Imperatives: *Seek, suffer, endure.* The Roman
In him feared the Law and told him where to stop.

So perfect a disguise for one who had
Exhausted death in art—yet who could guess
You would discern the liar by a line,
The suffering hidden under gentleness
And add upon the flyleaf in your tall
Clear hand: 'Fat, human and unloved,
And held from loving by a sort of wall,
Laid down his books and lovers one by one,
Indifference and success had crowned them all.'

HELOISE AND ABELARD

Heloise and Abelard
Nature's great hermaphrodites,
Artists in the human way,
Turned their sad endearing eyes,
Passionate and tiger-bright,
Closed the animal.
Yet in deprivation found
By a guess
Love unseal its loveliness.

Patents of their time and sex,
Body's rude containers
With their humours up like wicks,
Passionate and tiger-bright,
Made them foreigners
To themselves while still awake.
Yet with this he lights the stake
Feeds like faggots tied
Innocence and pride,
Bits of what had died.

Tombs may lie by two and two
On the Jordan's bends;
Death's unshrinking little noun
Marks them for his own,
The passionate and tiger-bright
Couples in their shadows lie
Till the action ends.
Death by lovelessness for these
Was unselaed in mysteries
By the enduring Friend.

Lucky who can sort out
The barren and the sown,
Whose punishments are given joy,
Who their own bodies own.
Who can discriminate,
Under reason's cruel rod
Between the friend in them
And enemy of God.

FABRE

The ants that passed
Over the back of his hand,
The cries of welcome, the tribes, the tribes!

Happier men would have studied
Children, more baffling than pupae,
Their conversation when alone, their voices,

The dream at the tea-table or at geography:
The sense of intimacy when moving in lines
Like caterpillars entering a cathedral.

He refused to examine the world except
Through the stoutest glasses;
A finger of ground covered with pioneers.

A continent on a bay-leaf moving.
If real women were like moths he didn't notice.
There was not a looking-glass in the whole house.

Ah! but one day he might dress
In this black discarded business suit,
Fly heavily out on to the lawn at Arles.

What friendships lay among the flowers!
If he could be a commuter among the bees,
This pollen-hunter of the exact observation!

POGGIO

The rubber penis, the wig, the false breasts . . .
The talent for entering rooms backwards
Upon a roar of laughter, with his dumb
Pained expression, wheeling there before him
That mythological great hippo's bum:

'Who should it be but Poggio?' The white face,
Comical, flat, and hairless as a cheese.
Nose like a member: something worn:
A Tuscan fig, a leather can, or else,
A phallus made of putty and slapped on.

How should you know that behind
All this the old buffoon concealed a fear—
And reasonable enough—that he might be
An artist after all? Always after this kind
Of side-splitting evening, sitting there
On a three-legged stool and writing, he

Hoped poems might form upon the paper.
But no. Dirty stories. The actress and the bishop.
The ape and the eunuch. This crapula clung
To him for many years between his dinners . . .
He sweated at them like a ham unhung.

And like the rest of us hoped for
The transfigured story or the mantic line
Of poetry free from this mortuary smell.
For years slept badly—who does not?
Took bribes, and drugs, ate far too much and dreamed.
Married unwisely, yes, but died quite well.

CONON THE CRITIC ON THE SIX LANDSCAPE PAINTERS OF GREECE

ON PETER OF THEBES

'This landscape is not original in its own mode. First smells were born—of resin and pine. Then someone got drunk on arbutus berries. Finally as an explanatory text someone added this red staunch clay and roots. You cannot smell one without tasting the other—as with fish and red sauce.'

ON MANOLI OF CRETE

'After a lifetime of writing acrostics he took up a brush and everything became twice as attentive. Trees had been trees before. Distinctions had been in ideas. Now the old man went mad, for everything undressed and ran laughing into his arms.'

ON JULIAN OF ARCADIA

'Arcadia is original in a particular sense. There is no feeling of "Therefore" in it. Origin, reason, meaning it has none in the sense of recognizable past. In this, both Arcadia and all good poems are original.'

ON SPIRIDON OF EPIRUS

'You look at this landscape for five years. You see little but something attentive watching you. Another five and you remark a shape that is barely a shape; a shadow like the moon's penumbra. Look a lifetime and you will see that the mountains lie like the covers of a bed; and you discern the form lying under them.'

ON HERO OF CORINTH

'Style is the cut of the mind. Hero was not much interested in his landscape, but by a perpetual self-confession in art removed both himself and his subject out of the reach of the people. Thus one day there remained only a picture-frame, an empty studio, and an idea of Hero the painter.'

ON ALEXANDER OF ATHENS

'Alexander was in love with Athens. He was a glutton and exhausted both himself and his subject in his art. Thus when he had smelt a flower it was quite used up, and when he painted a mountain it felt that living on could only be a useless competition against Alexander's painting of it. Thus with him Athens ceased to exist, and we have been walking about inside his canvases ever since looking for a way back from art into life.'

TWO POEMS IN BASIC ENGLISH

I

SHIPS. ISLANDS. TREES

These ships, these islands, these simple trees
Are our rewards in substance, being poor.
This earth a dictionary is
To the root and growth of seeing,
And to the servant heart a door.
Some on the green surface of the land
With all their canvas up in leaf and flower,
And some empty of influence
But from the water-winds,
Free as love's green attractions are.

Smoke bitter and blue from farms.
And points of feeble light in houses
Come after them in the scale
Of the material and the beautiful;
Are not less complex but less delicate
And less important than these living
Instruments of space,
Whose quiet communication is
With older trees in ships on the grey waves:
An order and a music
Like a writing on the skies
Too private for the reason or the pen;
Too simple even for the heart's surprise.

II

This rough field of sudden war—
This sand going down to the sea, going down,
Was made without the approval of love,
By a general death in the desire for living.
Time got the range of impulse here:
On old houses with no thought of armies,
Burnt guns, maps and firing:
All the apparatus of man's behaviour
Put by in memories for books on history:
A growth like these bitter
Green bulbs in the hollow sand here.
But ideas and language do not go.
The rate of the simple things—
Men walking here, thinking of houses,
Gardens, or green mountains or beliefs:
Units of the dead in these living armies,
Making comparison of this bitter heat,
And the living sea, giving up its bodies,
Level and dirty in the mist,
Heavy with sponges and the common error.

IN EUROPE

RECITATIVE FOR A RADIO PLAY

*Three Voices to the accompaniment of a drum and
bells, and the faint grunt and thud of a dancing bear.*

MAN

The frontiers at last, I am feeling so tired.
We are getting the refugee habit,

WOMAN

Moving from island to island,
Where the boundaries are clouds,
Where the frontiers of the land are water.

OLD MAN

We are getting the refugee habit,

WOMAN

We are only anonymous feet moving,
Without friends any more, without books
Or companionship any more. We are getting—

MAN

The refugee habit. There's no end
To the forest and no end to the moors:
Between the just and the unjust
There is little distinction.

OLD MAN

Bodies like houses, without windows and doors:

177

WOMAN

The children have become so brown,
Their skins have become dark with sunlight,

MAN

They have learned to eat standing.

OLD MAN

When we come upon men crucified,
Or women hanging downward from the trees,
They no longer understand.

WOMAN

How merciful is memory with its fantasies.
They are getting the refugee habit . . .

OLD MAN

How weary are the roads of the blood.
Walking forwards towards death in my mind
I am walking backwards again into my youth;
A mother, a father, and a house.
One street, a certain town, a particular place:
And the feeling of belonging somewhere,
Of being appropriate to certain fields and trees.

WOMAN

Now our address is the world. Walls
Constrain us. O do you remember
The peninsula where we so nearly died,
And the way the trees looked owned,
Human and domestic like a group of horses?
They said it was Greece.

MAN

Through Prussia into Russia,
Through Holland to Poland,
Through Rumania into Albania.

WOMAN

Following the rotation of the seasons.

OLD MAN

We are getting the refugee habit:
The past and the future are not enough,
Are two walls only between which to die:
Who can live in a house with two walls?

MAN

The present is an eternal journey;
In one country winter, in another spring.

OLD MAN

I am sick of the general deaths:
We have seen them impersonally dying:
Everything I had hoped for, fireside and hearth,
And death by compromise some summer evening.

MAN

You are getting the refugee habit:
You are carrying the past in you
Like a precious vessel, remembering
Its essence, ownership and ordinary loving.

WOMAN

We are too young to remember.

179

OLD MAN

Nothing disturbed such life as I remember
But telephone or telegram,
Such death-bringers to the man among the roses
In the garden of his house, smoking a pipe.

WOMAN

We are the dispossessed, sharing
With gulls and flowers our lives of accident:
No time for love, no room for love:
If only the children—

MAN

Were less wild and unkept, belonged
To the human family, not speechless,

OLD MAN

And shy as the squirrels in the trees:

WOMAN

If only the children

OLD MAN

Recognized their father, smiled once more.

OLD MAN + WOMAN

They have got the refugee habit,
Walking about in the rain for food,
Looking at their faces in the bottom of wells:

OLD MAN

They are living the popular life.
All Europe is moving out of winter
Into spring with all boundaries being
Broken down, dissolving, vanishing.
Migrations are beginning, a new habit
From where the icebergs rise in the sky
To valleys where corn is spread like butter . . .

WOMAN

So many men and women: each one a soul.

MAN

So many souls crossing the world,

OLD MAN

So many bridges to the end of the world.
Frontiers mean nothing any more . . .

WOMAN

Peoples and possessions,
Lands, rights,
Titles, holdings,
Trusts, Bonds. . . .

OLD MAN

Mean nothing any more, nothing.
A whistle, a box, a shawl, a cup,
A broken sword wrapped in newspaper.

WOMAN

All we have left us, out of context,

OLD MAN

A jar, a mousetrap, a broken umbrella,
A coin, a pipe, a pressed flower

WOMAN

To make an alphabet for our children.

OLD MAN

A chain, a whip, a lock,
A drum and a dancing bear . . .

WOMAN

We have got the refugee habit.
Beyond tears at last, into some sort of safety
From fear of wanting, fear of hoping,
Fear of everything but dying.
We can die now.

OLD MAN

Frontiers mean nothing any more. Dear Greece!

MAN

Yes. We can die now.

LETTER TO SEFERIS THE GREEK

'Ego dormio sed cor meum vigilat'

No milestones marked the invaders,
But ragged harps like mountains here:
A text for Proserpine in tears: worlds
With no doors for heroes and no walls with ears:
Yet snow, the anniversary of death.

How did they get here? How enact
This clear severe repentance on a rock,
Where only death converts and the hills
Into a pastoral silence by a lake,
By the blue Fact of the sky forever?

'Enter the dark crystal if you dare
And gaze on Greece.' They came
Smiling, like long reflections of themselves
Upon a sky of fancy. The red shoes
Waited among the thickets and the springs,
In fields of unexploded asphodels,
Neither patient nor impatient, merely
Waited, the born hunter on his ground,
The magnificent and funny Greek.

We will never record it: the black
Choirs of water flowing on moss,
The black sun's kisses opening,
Upon their blindness, like two eyes
Enormous, open in bed against one's own.

183

Something sang in the firmament.
The past, my friend compelled you,
The charge of habit and love.
The olive in the blood awoke,
The stones of Athens in their pride
Will remember, regret and often bless.

Kisses in letter from home:
Crosses in the snow: now surely
Lover and loved exist again
By a strange communion of darkness.
Those who went in all innocence,
Whom the wheel disfigured: whom
Charity will not revisit or repair,
The innocent who fell like apples.

Consider how love betrays us:
In the conversation of the prophets
Who daily repaired the world
By profit and loss, with no text
On the unknown quantity
By whose possession all problems
Are only ink and air made words:
I mean friends everywhere who smile
And reach out their hands.

Anger inherits where love
Betrays: iron only can clean:
And praises only crucify the loved
In their matchless errand, death.
Remember the earth will roll
Down her old grooves and spring
Utter swallows again, utter swallows.

Others will inherit the sea-shell,
Murmuring to the foolish its omens,
Uncurving on the drum of the ear,
The vowels of an ocean beyond us,
The history, the inventions of the sea:
Upon all parallels of the salt wave,
To lovers lying like sculptures
In islands of smoke and marble,
Will enter the reflections of poets
By the green wave, the chemical water.

I have no fear for the land
Of the dark heads with aimed noses,
The hair of night and the voices
Which mimic a traditional laughter:
Nor for a new language where
A mole upon a dark throat
Of a girl is called 'an olive':
All these things are simply Greece.

Her blue boundaries are
Upon a curving sky of time,
In a dark menstruum of water:
The names of islands like doors
Open upon it: the rotting walls
Of the European myth are here
For us, the industrious singers,
In the service of this blue, this enormous blue.

Soon it will be spring. Out of
This huge magazine of flowers, the earth,
We will enchant the house with roses,

The girls with flowers in their teeth,
The olives full of charm: and all of it
Given: can one say that
Any response is enough for those
Who have a woman, an island and a tree?

I only know that this time
More than ever, we must bless
And pity the darling dead: the women
Winding up their hair into sea-shells,
The faces of meek men like dials,
The great overture of the dead playing,
Calling all lovers everywhere in all stations
Who lie on the circumference of ungiven kisses.

Exhausted rivers ending in the sand;
Windmills of the old world winding
And unwinding in musical valleys your arms.
The contemptible vessel of the body lies
Lightly in its muscles like a vine;
Covered the nerves: and like an oil expressed
From the black olive between rocks,
Memory lulls and bathes in its dear reflections.

Now the blue lantern of the night
Moves on the dark in its context of stars.
O my friend, history with all her compromises
Cannot disturb the circuit made by this,
Alone in the house, a single candle burning
Upon a table in the whole of Greece.

Your letter of the 4th was no surprise.
So Tonio had gone? He will have need of us.
The sails are going out over the old world.
Our happiness, here on a promontory,
Marked by a star, is small but perfect.
The calculations of the astronomers, the legends
The past believed in could not happen here.
Nothing remains but Joy, the infant Joy
(So quiet the mountain in its shield of snow,
So unconcerned the faces of the birds),
With the unsuspected world somewhere awake,
Born of this darkness, our imperfect sight,
The stirring seed of Nostradamus' rose.

DAPHNIS AND CHLOE

This boy is the good shepherd.
He paces the impartial horizons,
Forty days in the land of tombs,
Waterless wilderness, seeking waterholes:
Knows the sound of the golden eagle, knows
The algebraic flute blue under Jupiter:
Supine in myrtle, lamb between his knees,
Has been a musical lion upon the midnight.

This was the good shepherd, Daphnis,
Time's ante-room by the Aegean tooth,
Curled like an umber snake above the spray,
Mumbling arbutus among the chalk-snags,
The Grecian molars where the green sea spins,
Suffered a pastoral decay.

This girl was the milk and the honey.
Under the eaves the dark figs ripen,
The leaves nine medicines, a climbing wine.
Under the tongue the bee-sting,
Under the breast the adder at the lung,
Like feathered child at wing.

Life's honey is distilled simplicity:
The icy crystal pendant from the rock,
The turtle's scorching ambush for the egg,
The cypress and the cicada,
And wine-dark, blue, and curious, then,
The metaphoric sea.

This was Chloe, the milk and honey,
Carved in the clear geography of Time,
The skeleton clean chiselled out in chalk,
For our Nigerian brown to study on.
From the disease of life, took the pure way,
Declined into the cliffs, the European waters,
Suffered a pastoral decay.

THE HANGED MAN

From this glass gallows in famous entertainment,
Upside down and by the dust yellowed,
The hanged man considers a green county,
Hallowed by gallows on a high hill.

The rooks of his two blue eyes eating
A mineral diet, that smile not while
The invaders move: on the dark down there
Owls with soft scissors cherish him.

Yellower than plantains by the dust touched
These hands in their chamber-music turning,
As viol or cello, these might easily be
The sullen fingers of a fallen Charles.

So will the horseman speculate in his cloak,
The felloes of the wagon cease their screech,
While one widens the eye of the farm-girl
Telling how rope ripens on a high hill.

SUMMER

The little gold cigale
Is summer's second god, the lovers know it,
His parched reverberating voice
Deepens the gold thirst of the noons
And follows the black sun's long
Fig-ripening and vine-mellowing fall
So leisurely from heaven's golden car
Day by successive day to end it all . . .

And where the Latin heat has stretched
The skin of valleys will his voice
Rubbing and scraping at the lover's ear
Oracles of past suns recall,
Prodigals of leisure and brown skins,
Wine mixed with kisses and the old
Dreamless summer sleeps they once enjoyed
In Adam's Eden long before the Fall.

IN CRISIS

My love on Wednesday letting fall her body
From upright walking won by weariness,
As on a bed of flesh by ounces counted out,
Softer than snuff or snow came where my body was.

So in the aboriginal waterways of the mind,
No word being spoken by a familiar girl,
One may have a clear apprehension of ghostly matters,
Audible, as perhaps in the sea-shell's helix.

The Gulf Stream can rub soft music from a pebble
Like quiet rehearsal of the words 'Kneel down':
And cool on the inner corridors of the ear
Can blow on memory and conscience like a sin.

The inner man is surely a native of God
And his wife a brilliant novice of nature.
The woman walks in the dark like a lantern swung,
A white spark blown between points of pain.

We do not speak, embracing with the blood,
The tolling heart marking its measures in darkness
Like the scratch of a match or the fire-stone
Struck to a spark in the dark by a colder one.

So, lying close, the enchanted boy may hear
Soon from Tokio the crass drum sounding,
From the hero's hearth the merry crotchet of war.
Flame shall swallow the lady.

192

Tall men shall come to cool the royal bush,
Over the grey waters the bugler's octaves
Publish aloud a new resurrection of terror.
Many will give suck at the bomb's cold nipple.

Empty your hearts: or fill from a purer source.
That what is in men can weep, having eyes:
That what is in Truth can speak from the responsible dust
And O the rose grow in the middle of the great world.

A NOCTUARY IN ATHENS

I

I have tasted my quantum of misfortune,
Have prayed before the left-handed woman;

Now as the rain of heaven downfalling tastes of space,
So the swimmer in the ocean of self, alone,

Utters his journey like a manual welcome,
Sculptures his element in search of grace.

II

I have sipped from the flask of resurrection,
Have eaten the oaten cake of redemption,

And love, sweet love, who weeps by the water-clock
Can bring if she will the sexton and the box,

For I wear my age as wood wears voluble leaves,
The temporal hunger and the carnal locks.

III

I have buried my wife under a dolmen,
Where others sleep as naked as the clouds,

Where others lie and weigh their dreams by ounces,
Where tamarisk, lentisk lean to utter sweets,

And angels in their shining moods retire:
Where from the wells the voice of truth pronounces.

194

IV

I have tasted my quantum of misfortune.
In the desert, the cities of ash and feathers,

In front of others I have spoken the vowel,
Knelt to the curly wool, the uncut horns;

Have carried my tribulation in a basket of wattle,
Solitary in my penitence as the owl.

V

I have set my wife's lip under the bandage,
O pound the roses, bind the eye of the soul,

Recite the charm of the deep and heal soon,
For the mountains accuse, and the sky's walls.

Let the book of sickness be put in the embers.
I have tasted my quantum of misfortune.

ADAM

I have nibbled the mystical fruit. Cover me.
Lest the prophetic fish follow and swallow me.
I dare not tread among the lilies
Though lambswool cover my footfall,
Though the adder call, the Word walk,
In the orchard voices follow, hands hallow me.

Thy will be done as it was in Eden.
We were a long time—I am afraid—
Naked among silver fish and shadows,
A long time and in silence naked. Only
The fountains falling, the hornet's drum
Calling, sunny and drunk with dew.

I am Adam, of singular manufacture,
A little clay, water, and prophetic breath;
On the waters of chaos a lamp of red clay.
The Word owns me. I have no armament
Only my fear of the walking Thing.

The rib follows me everywhere: and everywhere
A shadow follows the rib. Eve,
I am afraid. The Host walks and talks
In the baobab shade: the unknowable Thing
Is crossing the paths: the breath, woman,
Is on us: a white light: O cover me
From the unthinkable razor of thought
Whose whisper hangs over me.

Eve, we are in this thing to the very end,
You, your shadow, and shadowless Adam, I.
O rib and morsel of anguish, bone of contention,
After the thing has shone and gone,
After it enters the terrible wood,
We will win through, perhaps: cover us deep
Beyond clue with the leaves of the wood:
Be silent until it passes: and kiss me, kiss me.
Ah! but the apple, the apple was good!

SELF TO NOT-SELF

Darkness, divulge my share in light
As man in name though not in nature.
Lay down truth's black hermetic wings
For less substantial things
To call my weight my own
By love's nomenclature:
Matriculate by harmlessness
From this tuistic zone,
Possessing what I almost own.

And where each heap of music falls
Burns like a star below the sea
To light the ocean's cracked saloons
And mirror its plurality
Through nature's tideless nights and noons
Teach me the mastery of the curse,
The bending circumstance to free,
And mix my better with my worse.

CITIES, PLAINS AND PEOPLE

I

Once in idleness was my beginning,

Night was to the mortal boy
Innocent of surface like a new mind
Upon whose edges once he walked
In idleness, in perfect idleness.

O world of little mirrors in the light.
The sun's rough wick for everybody's day:
Saw the Himalayas like lambs there
Stir their huge joints and lay
Against his innocent thigh a stony thigh.

Combs of wind drew through this grass
To bushes and pure lakes
On this tasteless wind
Went leopards, feathers fell or flew:
Yet all went north with the prayer-wheel,
By the road, the quotation of nightingales.

Quick of sympathy with springs
Where the stone gushed water
Women made their water like thieves.

Caravans paused here to drink Tibet.
On draughty corridors to Lhasa
Was my first school
In faces lifted from saddles to the snows:
Words caught by the soft klaxons crying
Down to the plains and settled cities.

So once in idleness was my beginning.
Little known of better then or worse
But in the lens of this great patience
Sex was small,
Death was small,
Were qualities held in a deathless essence,
Yet subjects of the wheel, burned clear
And immortal to my seventh year.

To all who turn and start descending
The long sad river of their growth:
The tidebound, tepid, causeless
Continuum of terrors in the spirit,
I give you here unending
In idleness an innocent beginning

Until your pain become a literature.

II

Nine marches to Lhasa.

Those who went forward
Into this honeycomb of silence often
Gained the whole world: but often lost each other.
In the complexion of this country tears
Found no harbour in the breast of rock.
Death marched beside the living as a friend
With no sad punctuation by the clock.

But he for whom steel and running water
Were roads, went westward only
To the prudish cliffs and the sad green home
Of Pudding Island o'er the Victorian foam.

Here all as poets were pariahs.
Some sharpened little follies into hooks
To pick upon the language and survive.
Some in search could only found
Pulpits of smoke like Blake's *Jerusalem*.

For this person it was never landfall,
With so many representative young men
And all the old being obvious in feeling,
But like good crafty men

He saw the business witches in their bowlers,
The blackened Samsons of the green estate,
The earls from their cockney-boxes calling,
And knew before it was too late, London
Could only be a promise-giving kingdom.

Yet here was a window
Into the great sick-room, Europe,
With its dull set-books,
The Cartesian imperatives, Dante and Homer,
To impress the lame and awkward newcomer.

Here he saw Bede who softly
Blew out desire and went to bed,
So much greater than so many less
Who made their unconquered guilt in atrophy
A passport to the dead.

Here St. Augustine took the holy cue
Of bells in an English valley; and mad Jerome
Made of his longing half a home from home.

Scythes here faithfully mark
In their supple practice paths
For the lucky and unambitious owners.
But not a world as yet. Not a world.

Death like autumn falls
On the lakes its sudden forms, on walls
Where everything is made more marginal
By the ruling planes of the snow;
Reflect how Prospero was born to a green cell
While those who noted the weather-vane
In Beatrice's shadow sang
With the dying Emily: 'We shall never
Return, never be young again'.

The defeat of purpose in days and lichens.
Some here unexpectedly put on the citizen,
Go walking to a church
By landscape rubbed in rain to grey
As wool on glass,
Thinking of spring which never comes to stay.

(The potential passion hidden, Wordsworth
In the desiccated bodies of postmistresses.
The scarlet splash of campion, Keats.
Ignorant suffering that closes like a lock.)

So here at last we did outgrow ourselves.
As the green stalk is taken from the earth,
With a great juicy sob, I turned him from a Man
To Mandrake, in Whose awful hand I am.

III

Prospero upon his island
Cast in a romantic form,
When his love was fully grown
He laid his magic down.

Truth within the tribal wells,
Innocent inviting creature
Does not rise to human spells
But by paradox

Teaches all who seek for her
That no saint or seer unlocks
The wells of truth unless he first
Conquer for the truth his thirst.

IV

So one fine year to where the roads
Dividing Europe meet in Paris.

The gnome was here and the small
Unacted temptations. Tessa was here whose dark
Quickened hair had brushed back rivers,
Trembling with stars by Buda,

In whose inconstant arms he waited
For black-hearted Descartes to seek him out
With all his sterile apparatus.
Now man for him became a thinking lobe,
Through endless permutations sought repose.
By frigid latinisms he mated now
To the hard frame of prose the cogent verb.

To many luck may give for merit
More profitable teachers. To the heart
A critic and a nymph:
And an unflinching doctor to the spirit.

All these he confined in metaphors,
She sleeping in his awkward mind
Taught of the pace of women or birds
Through the leafy body of man
Enduring like the mammoth, like speech
From the dry clicking of the greater apes
To these hot moments in a reference of stars
Beauty and death, how sex became
A lesser sort of speech, and the members doors.

V

Faces may settle sadly
Each into its private death
By business travel or fortune,
Like the fat congealing on a plate
Or the fogged negative of labour
Whose dumb fastidious rectitude
Brings death in living as a sort of mate.

Here however man might botch his way
To God via Valéry, Gide or Rabelais.
All rules obtain upon the pilot's plan
So long as man, not manners, makyth man.
Some like the great Victorians of the past
Through old Moll Flanders sailed before the mast,
While savage Chatterleys of the new romance
Get carried off in Sex, the ambulance.
All rules obtain upon the pilot's chart
If governed by the scripture of the heart.

VI

Now November visiting with rain
Surprises and humbles with its taste of elsewhere,
Licks in the draughty galleries there,
Like a country member quickened by a province,
Turning over books and leaves in haste,
Takes at last her slow stains of waste
Down the stone stairs into the rivers.

And in the personal heart, weary
Of the piercing innocents in parks
Who sail the rapt subconscious there like swans,
Disturbs and brightens with her tears, thinking:

'Perhaps after all it is we who are blind,
While the unconscious eaters of the apple
Are whole as ingots of a process
Punched in matter by the promiscuous Mind.'

VII

By the waters of Buda
We surrendered arms, hearts, hands,
Lips for counting of kisses,
Fingers for money or touch,
Eyes for the hourglass sands.

Uncut and unloosened
Swift hair by the waters of Buda
In the shabby balcony rooms
Where the pulses waken and wonder
The churches bluff one as heart-beats
On the river their dull boom booms.

By the waters of Buda
Uncomb and unlock then,
Abandon and nevermore cherish
Queer lips, queer heart, hands.
There to futurity leave
The luckier lover who's waiting,
As, like a spring coiled up,
In the bones of Adam, lay Eve.

VIII

So Time, the lovely and mysterious
With promises and blessings moves
Through her swift degrees,
So gladly does he bear
Towards the sad perfect wife,
The rocky island and the cypress-trees.

Taken in the pattern of all solitaries,
An only child, of introspection got,
Her only playmates, lovers, in herself.
Nets were too coarse to hold her
Where the nymph broke through
And only the encircling arms of pleasure held.

Here for the five lean dogs of sense
Greece moved in calm memorial
Through her own unruffled blue,
Bearing in rivers upside down
The myrtle and the olive, in ruins
The faces of the innocents in wells.

Salt and garlic, water and dry bread,
Greek bread from the comb they knew
Like an element in sculpture:
By these red aerial cherries,
Or flawed grapes painted green
But pouted into breasts: as well
By those great quarries of the blood—
The beating crimson hearts of the grenades:
All far beyond the cupidity of verses
Or the lechery of images to tell.

Here worlds were confirmed in him.

Differences that matched like cloth
Between the darkness and the inner light,
Moved on the undivided breath of blue.
Formed moving, trees asserted here
Nothing but simple comparisons to
The artist's endearing eye.

Sleep. Napkins folded after grace.

Veins of stealing water
By the unplumbed ruins, never finding peace.
A watershed, a valley of tombs,
Never finding peace.

'Look' she might say 'Press here
With your fingers at the temples.
Are they not the blunt uncut horns
Of the small naked Ionian fauns?'

Much later, moving in a dark,
Snow-lit landscape softly
In her small frock walked his daughter
And a simile came into his mind
Of lovers, like swimmers lost at sea,
Exhausted in each other's arms,
Urgent for land, but treading water.

IX

Red Polish mouth,
Lips that as for the flute unform,
Gone round on nouns or vowels,
To utter the accepting, calm
'Yes', or make terrible verbs
Like 'I adore, adore'.

Persuader, so long hunted
By your wild pack of selves,
Past peace of mind or even sleep,

So longed for and so sought,
May the divider always keep
Like unshed tears in lashes
Love, the undeclarèd thought.

X

Now earth turns her cold shoulders to us,
Autumn with her wild packs
Comes down to the robbing of the flowers.
On this unstained sky, printless
Snow moves crisp as dreamers' fingers,
And the rate of passion or tenderness
In this island house is absolute.

Within a time of reading
Here is all my growth
Through the bodies of other selves,
In books, by promise or perversity
My mutinous crew of furies—their pleading
Threw up at last the naked sprite
Whose flesh and noise I am,
Who is my jailor and my inward night.

In Europe, bound by Europe,
I saw them moving, the possessed
Fëdor and Anna, the last
Two vain explorers of our guilt,
Turn by turn holding the taws,
Made addicts of each other lacking love,
Friendless embittered and alone.

The lesser pities held them back
Like mice in secrecies,
Yet through introspection and disease,
Held on to the unflinching bone,
The sad worn ring of Anna,
Loyal to filth and weakness,
Hammered out on this slender bond,
Fëdor's raw cartoons and episodes.
By marriage with this ring,
Companioned each their darkness.
In cracked voices we can hear
These hideous mommets now
Like westering angels over Europe sing.

XI

So knowledge has an end,
And virtue at the last an end,
In the dark field of sensibility
The unchanging and unbending;
As in aquariums gloomy
On the negative's dark screen
Grow the shapes of other selves,
So groaned for by the heart,
So seldom grasped if seen.

Love bears you. Time stirs you.
Music at midnight makes a ground,
Or words on silence so perplex
In hidden meanings there like bogies
Waiting the expected sound.

Art has limits and life limits
Within the nerves that support them.

So better with the happy
Discover than with the wise
Who teach the sad valour
Of endurance through the seasons,
In change the unchanging
Death by compromise.

XII

Now darkness comes to Europe
Dedicated by a soft unearthly jazz.
The greater hearts contract their joys
By silence to the very gem,
While the impertinent reformers,
Barbarians with secretaries move,
Whom old Cavafy pictured,
Whom no war can remove.

Through the ambuscades of sex,
The follies of the will, the tears,
Turning, a personal world I go
To where the yellow emperor once
Sat out the summer and the snow,
And searching in himself struck oil,
Published the first great Tao
Which all confession can only gloze
And in the Consciousness can only spoil
Apparent opposition of the two
Where unlocked numbers show their fabric,

He laid his finger to the map,
And where the signs confuse,
Defined the Many and the None
As base reflections of the One.

What bifid Hamlet in the maze
Wept to find; the *doppelgänger*
Goethe saw one morning go
Over the hill ahead; the man
So gnawed by promises who shared
The magnificent responses of Rimbaud.
All that we have sought in us,
The artist by his greater cowardice
In sudden brush-strokes gave us clues—
Hamlet and Faust as front-page news.
The yellow emperor first confirmed
By one Unknown the human calculus,
Where feeling and idea,
Must fall within this space,
This personal landscape built
Within the Chinese circle's calm embrace.

Dark Spirit, sum of all
That has remained unloved,
Gone crying through the world:
Source of all manufacture and repair,
Quicken the giving-spring
In ferns and birds and ordinary people
That all deeds done may share,
By this our temporal sun,
The part of living that is loving,
Your dancing, a beautiful behaviour.

Darkness, who contain
The source of all this corporal music,
On the great table of the Breath
Our opposites in pity bear,
Our measure of perfection or of pain,
Both trespassers in you, that then
Our Here and Now become your Everywhere.

XIII

The old yellow Emperor
With defective sight and matted hair
His palace fell to ruins
But his heart was in repair.

Veins like imperfect plumbing
On his flesh described a leaf.
His palms were mapped with cunning
Like geodesies of grief.

His soul became a vapour
And his limbs became a stake
But his ancient heart still visits us
In Lawrence or in Blake.

XIV

All cities plains and people
Reach upwards to the affirming sun,
All that's vertical and shining,
Lives well lived,
Deeds perfectly done,
Reach upwards to the royal pure
Affirming sun.

Accident or error conquered
By the gods of luck or grace,
Form and face,
Tribe or caste or habit,
All are aspects of the one
Affirming race.

Ego, my dear, and id
Lie so profoundly hid
In space-time void, though feeling,
While contemporary, slow,
We conventional lovers cheek to cheek
Inhaling and exhaling go.

The rose that Nostradamus
In his divining saw
Break open as the world;
The city that Augustine
Founded in moral law,
By our anguish were compelled
To urge, to beckon and implore.

Dear Spirit, should I reach,
By touch or speech corrupt,
The inner suffering word,
By weakness or idea,
Though you might suffer
Feel and know,
Pretend you do not hear.

XV

Bombers bursting like pods go down
And the seed of Man stars
This landscape, ancient but no longer known.
Only the critic perseveres
Within his ant-like formalism
By deduction and destruction steers;
Only the trite reformer holds his own.

See looking down motionless
How clear Athens or Bremen seem
A mass of rotten vegetables
Firm on the diagram of earth can lie;
And here you may reflect how *genus epileptoid*
Knows his stuff; and where rivers
Have thrown their switches and enlarged
Our mercy or our knowledge of each other;
Wonder who walks beside them now and why,
And what they talk about.

There is nothing to hope for, my Brother.
We have tried hoping for a future in the past.
Nothing came out of that past
But the reflected distortion and some
Enduring, and understanding, and some brave.
Into their cool embrace the awkward and the sinful
Must be put for they alone
Know who and what to save.

Small temptations now—to slumber and to sleep,
Where the lime-green, odourless
And pathless island waters
Crossing and uncrossing, partnerless
By hills alone and quite incurious
Their pastures of reflection keep.

For Prospero remains the evergreen
Cell by the margin of the sea and land,
Who many cities, plains, and people saw
Yet by his open door
In sunlight fell asleep
One summer with the Apple in his hand.

Beirut

'A SOLILOQUY OF HAMLET'

(*to Anne Ridler*)

I

Here on the curve of the embalming winter,
Son of the three-legged stool and the Bible,

By the trimmed lamp I cobble this sonnet
For father, son, and the marble woman.

Sire, we have found no pardonable city
Though women harder than the kneeling nuns,

Softer than clouds upon the stones of pain,
Have breathed their blessings on a candle-end.

Some who converted the English oak-trees:
The harmless druids singing in green places.

Some who broke their claws upon islands:
The singing fathers in the boats of glory.

Some who made an atlas of their hunger:
The enchanted skulls lie under the lion's paw.

II

One innocent observer in a foreign cell
Died when my father lay beside his ghost.

Dumb poison in the hairy ear of kings
Can map the nerves and halt the tick of hearts.

The phoenix burning at his window-sill
Put peace around him like a great basin.

So whether the ocean curved beneath his dreams
On floors full of the sea-shell's music,

His privacy aims like a pointed finger:
Death grows like poison-ivy on a stick.

Truly his unruly going grows like a green wand
Between the broken pavements of the heart,

And all whose blood ticks fast at funerals
Must dread the tapping of the vellum drum.

III

Guilt can lie heavier than house of tortoise.
Winter and love, O desperate medicines,

Under the turf we bless the wishing spring,
The seed from the index-finger of the saint.

To the snow I sing out this hoarse prescription:
'Sweet love, from the enduring geometric egg,

An embryo grinning in its coloured cap,
O I walk under a house of horn, seeking a door.'

The charming groans of ladies come to me
From the nursery sills of an invented climate:

My outlawed mother patient at the loom,
Behind her, oaks, their nude machinery,

The dark ones shining on their snowy tuffets.
I take this image on a screaming nib.

IV

Here in the hollow curvature of the world,
Now time turns through her angles on a dial,

The unspeaking surgeon cuts beneath the fur,
And pain forever green winds her pale horn.

Make in the beautiful harbours of the heart,
For scholars sitting at their fire-lit puzzles,

The three-fold climate and the anchorage.
Make in the dormitory of the self

For sleepless murders combing out the blood
A blessing and an armistice to fear.

Though bankers pile debentures to the worm,
And death like Sunday only brings the owls

Though some must founder trying for the rock,
Bless mice and women in their secret places.

V

To you in high heaven the unattainable,
The surnamed Virgin, I lift a small scripture,

Brushed by the quill of a black boy's madness;
Pour one sweet drop of mercy on the mind!

You three, being holy and great linguists,
The oval singers of the Cretan eikon,

Give to the ghost your charity's ghostly shirt,
Defence by pity and a green captivity.

Consider: here the thorn crawled in the heart,
Here traitors laid an axe upon the root.

Grant like a bruise his sweetest homecoming,
Find laughing Hamlet sitting in a tree,

The silken duchess frowning at her baubles,
And swart Ophelia crooning at her lauds.

VI

Winter and love are Euclid's properties.
The charm of candles smoking on a coffin

Like nursery years upon a birthday cake,
Teach, like the soft declensions of the term,

How dust being sifted from the sheet of nuns,
Returns beneath the swollen veil once more,

So women bend like trees and utter figs,
And children from their pillows prophesy.

The unnumbered garrison still holds the womb.
O suffer the mirages of the dazed ladies,

Give love with all its tributary patience
That when the case of bones is broken open,

The heart can bless, or the sad skin of saints
Be beaten into drum-heads for the truth.

VII

Walk upon dreams, and pass behind the book.
Hamlet is nailed between the thieves of love.

Wear the black waistcoat, boy, for death is king,
His margin is a waxen candle-dip at night:

By day a grace-note in the mid of silence,
The gambler smiling in his royal sheet.

For this I put the obol in the lips.
For this I wear my sex beneath a towel.

I take the round skull of the nunnery girl
To bless until the tears break in the brain;

As those who by the Babylonian fable
Hung up their piercing harps beside the waters,

I hang my heart, being choked, upon a noun.
I hang her name upon this frantic pothook.

VIII

I close an hinge on the memorial days.
I perch my pity on an alp of silence.

Cold water took my pretty by the beard,
Flatter than glass she blew to the tongueless zone.

I learn now from nightingale on the spit
The science of the cowl and killing-bottle.

I hum now the harsh tune of the too finite swan,
Piping behind the ambush of my guilt.

My comfort smiled on me and gave me flowers:
Freckles, as on a sparrow's egg, and quiet faces.

The water strips her humour like a bean.
Barbarian ladies with their fingernails,

Strip off her simple reason like a wedding-dress.
She turns upon the pedals of her prison.

IX

Pain hangs more bloody than the mystic's taws.
Down corridors of pain I follow patience,

Make notes behind the nerve-ends of the brain.
Lean, lean on the iron elbow of the armoured man,

Button the nipples on his coat of mercy,
The widow walking in a rubber mask!

Your murderer's napkin hangs upon a bush,
And the king who stiffens in a shirt of blood,

Too good, too grave to number with the crumbs,
Can leave an incubus to this winter castle.

Shoot back the lips like bolts upon your grace.
Make thimble of the mouth to suck your fly.

I cool my spittle on the smoking hook.
I take these midnight thoughts between a tong.

X

As husband is laid down beside the lute,
Widow and minstrel in a single cerement,

So I on the plinth of passing, shall I marry
The lunatic image in the raven frock?

The curved meridian of hazard like a bow
Paints on the air the dark tree of my death

Gums without ivory for the skeletal smile:
A natal joker squeaking in his crib.

Here birth and death are knitted by a vowel.
A mariner must sail his crew of furies

Beyond the hook of hazard to the oceanic lands.
His prayers will bubble up before the throne.

I, now, go, where the soliloquy of the sad bee
O numbs the nettles and the hieroglyphic stone.

XI

On the stone sill of the embalming winter
I tell my malady by the wheel and the berry,

The hunters making their necklace on the hills.
The escaping dead hang frozen down like flags,

A breathing frost upon the eyeball lens
Blooms like still poison in a dish of quinces.

Spawn of the soft, the unwrinkled womb of queens,
I add my number to the world's defeated,

I learn the carrion's scientific torpor
The five-day baby swollen with its gases,

The nun who fell from the ladder of Jacob
My love hangs longer than the tongue of hound.

I kneel at the keyhole of death's private room
To meet His eye, enormous in the keyhole.

XII

This pain goes deeper than the fish's fathom.
Peel me an olive-branch and hold it shining:

You have Ophelia smiling at her chess,
The suit of love gored by the courtier's fang.

You have my mother folded like a rag,
Whiter than piano-keys the canine smile.

The marble statues bleed if she walks by,
Pacing the margins of the chequerboard

Where the soft rabbit and her man in black
Play move for move, the pawn against the prince.

O men have made cradles of their loving fingers
To rock my youth, and I have slipped between,

Led like the magi to the child's foul crib,
To hear my hands nailed up between two thieves.

XIII

Then walk where roses like disciples can
Aim at the heart their innocent attention.

Where the apostle-spring beneath the cover
Of throstle and dove, loves in his green asylum.

Time shall bestow a pupil to the nipple,
A red and popular baby born for the urn.

For him I make a book by the moving finger-bone,
A rattle, cap and comedy of queens.

Then suckle the weather if the winter will not,
Seal down a message in a dream of spring,

More than this painful meditation of feet,
The frigid autist pacing out his rope.

The candle and the lexicon have picked your bones.
The tallow spills upon my endless bible.

XIV

To you by whom the sweet spherical music
Makes in heaven a tree-stringed oracle,

I bend a sonnet like a begging-bowl,
And hang my tabor from the greenest willow-wand.

Give to the rufus sons of Pudding Island
The stainless sheet of a European justice,

That death's pure canon smiling in the trees
Can lure the fabulous lion from his walks.

My ash I dress to dance upon the void,
My mercy in a wallet like a berry bright,

And when hemp sings of murder bless your boy,
The double fellow in the labyrinth,

Whose maps were stifled with him in the maze,
Whose mother dropped him like the seedless pod.

THE DEATH OF GENERAL UNCEBUNKE

A BIOGRAPHY IN LITTLE

1938

(To Kay in Tahiti: now dead.)
'Not satire but an exercise in ironic compassion.'

FOURTEEN CAROLS

I

My uncle sleeps in the image of death.
In the greenhouse and in the potting-shed
The wrens junket: the old girl with the trowel
Is a pillar of salt, insufferably brittle.
His not to reason why, though a thinking man.
Beside his mesmeric incomprehension
The little mouse mopping and mowing,
The giraffe and the spin-turtle, these can
On my picture-book look insufferably little
But knowing, incredibly Knowing.

II

My uncle has gone beyond astronomy.
He sleeps in the music-room of the Host.
Voyage was always his entertainment
Who followed a crooked needle under Orion,
Saw the griffin, left notes on the baobab,
Charted the Yellow Coast.

228

He like a faultless liner, finer never took air,
But snow on the wings altered the altitude,
She paused in a hollow pocket, faltered:
The enormous lighted bird is dashed in snow.
Now in the labyrinth God will put him wise,
Correct the instruments, will alter even
The impetuous stance, the focus of the eyes.

III

Aunt Prudence, she was the eye of the needle.
Sleeping, a shepherdess of ghostly sheep.
'Thy will be done in Baden Baden.
In Ouchy, Lord, and in Vichy.'
In the garden of the vicarage sorting stamps
Was given merit of the poor in spirit
For dusting a cinquefoil, tuning the little lamps.

Well, God sends weather, the English apple,
The weeping willow.
Grum lies the consort of Prudence quite:
Mum as a long fiddle in regimentals:
This sudden IT between two tropical thumbs.
Unwrinkle him, Lord, unriddle this strange gorgon,
For tall Prudence who softens the small lamps,
Gives humble air to the organ that it hums.

IV

My uncle sleeps in the image of death.
Not a bad sport the boys will tell you,

229

More than a spartan in tartan.
Yet he, fearing neither God nor man,
Feared suffocation by marble,
Wrote a will in hexameters, burnt the cakes,
Came through with the cavalry, ladies from hell,
Feared neither God nor man,
Devoted to the polo-pony, mesmerized by stamps.

Now in the stable the hypnotic horse-flesh
Champ, stamp, yawn, paw in the straw,
And in the bedroom the blind warhorse
Gallops all night the dark fields of Dis.

V

My uncle has gone beyond astronomy.
His sleep is of the Babylonian deep-sea
Darker than bitumen, defter than devil's alliances.
He has seen Golgotha in carnival:
Now in the shin-bone the smart worm
Presides at the death of the sciences,
The Trinity sleeps in his knee.

Curse Orion who pins my man like moth,
Who sleeps in the monotony of his zone,
Who is a daft ankle-bone among stars,
O shame on the beggar by silent lands
Who has nothing but carbon for his own.

Uncouple the flutes! Strike with the black rod!
Our song is no more plural, the bones
Are hollow without your air, Lord God.
Give us the language of diamonds or
The speech of the little stones.

VI

Prudence shall cross also the great white barrier.
God shall fold finally up the great fan—
Benevolent wings wheeling over the rectory,
The vicar, the thatcher, the rat-catcher,
Sure in this medicine help her all they can.
O she is sure in step with the step of the Master.
Winter loosens the apple, fastens the Eskimo.
Wearing his pug-marks for slippers shall follow,
Holding to common prayer, the Great Bear;
Over the Poles, wherever his voyages go.

Shall navigate also the great circle,
Confer with the serious mammoth, the sabre-tooth,
Come to the sole goal, palace of higher things,
Where God's good silverware spills on all faces,
And hazardously the good wizard, gives wings.

VII

My uncle sleeps in the image of death.
He sleeps the steep sleep of his zone,
His downward tilting sleep beyond alarm.
Heu! he will come to harm so alone.

Who says for him the things he dare not say?
He cannot speak to angels from his rock.
This pediment of sleep is his impediment.
Grant him the speech of sleep,
Not this dank slag, the deathward sediment.
Strike with the rod, Lord God.
Here was a ruddy bareback man,
Emptied his blood upon the frozen lake,
Wheeled back the screaming mares,
Crossing the Jordan.

Excuse me, Lord God, numberer of hairs,
Sender of telegrams, the poisoned arrow,
Suffer your faithful hound, give him
At least the portion of the common sparrow.

VIII

My uncle has gone beyond astronomy.
Three, six, nine of the dead languages
Are folded under his lip.
He has crossed over into Tartary,
Burnt his boats, dragged the black ice for bodies,
Seen trees in the water, skippered God's little ship.

He is now luggage, excess baggage,
Not wanted on voyage, scaling a pass,
Or swinging a cutlass in the Caribbean,
Under Barbados chewing the frantic marsh-rice,
Seven dead men, a crooked foot, a cracked jaw,
Ten teeth like hollow dice.

232

My uncle is sleeping in economy.
No word is wasted for the common ghost
Speaks inwards: he lies in the status
Of death's dumb music, the dumb dead king
On an ivory coast.

IX

Prudence had no dog and but one cat,
Black of bonnet the Lord's plain precept saw
At the at-home, on Calvary, in the darkest nook
He was there; He leaned on a window smiling,
The God Shepherd crooking his ghostly crook.
Prudence did dip and delve in the Holy Book,
Alpha to omega angels told her the tale,
Feeding the parrot, pensive over a croquet-hoop:

'Once upon a time was boy and girl,
Living on cherry, berry, fisherman's silver catch.
Now the crass cock crows in the coop,
Prudence, the door dangles, lacking a latch.'

X

My uncle has gone beyond astronomy.
He sleeps the sharp sleep of the unstrung harp.
Crossed into Tartary, he lies deep
In the flora and fauna of death,
Under a black snowline sleeps the steep,
Botanical, plant-pure sleep.

233

The soul is folded like a little mouse.
Body is mortuary here, the clock
Foiled in its own wheels—but he may be sleeping,
Even if no toe moves no where, the sock
Be empty of all but vessels—where is he creeping?
Where is my man's address? How does he perish
Who was my relish, who was without fault?

Strike with the black rod, Lord God.
This is the marmoreal person, the rocky one.
This is the pillar of savourless salt.

XI

My uncle has gone beyond astronomy.
He sleeps in the pocket of Lapland,
Hears thunder on a Monday, has known
Bone burn to ash for the urn's hold.
He has fine nails of his finger and of his toe.
Now colder than spittle is his mettle. The hand
Is cold bone touching cold stone. So
In the sad womb he plays the trump of doom.

Lord, here is music. This fine white 'cello
Hums no more to the gust of your air.
This supercilious fellow, think what was given
To nourish his engine, salt barley and beer.
All wasted, gone over, destroyed by death's leaven,
Scent of the apple and stain of the berry.
Now only the ignorant hedgehog dare,
Smelling the fruit in him, dance and be merry.

XII

Prudence was told the tale of the chimney-corner
In the ingle beetled over the red troll's book
Ate the white lie: 'Happily ever after,
A hunchback, a thimble, a smart swan,
Ride time's tall wave, musically on and on . . .'
Was it of God to bait and wait with the hook?
Was it of him black laughter at 'happily ever after',
A grass widow, a shadow embalmed in a story-book?

Memory is morsels offered of sparrows.
First prize a jug and bowl for correcting the clock,
Sending a telegram, gathering holy campion.
Lowly Prue is glum of finger and thumb,
Toe in the ember, dismembering spools of knitting.
Patience on a monument, passion on a cushion.
God's champion darning a sock, sitting.

XIII

My uncle sleeps in the image of death.
The shadow of other worlds, deep-water penumbra
Covers his marble: he is past sighing,
Body a great slug there, a fine white
Pike in a green pond lying.
My uncle was a red man. The dead man
Knew to shoe horses: the habits of the owl,
Time of tillage, foison, cutting of lumber,
Like Saint Columba,
Could coax the squirrels into his cowl.

Heu! for the tombeau, the sombre flambeau,
Immanent with God he lies in Limbo.
Break punic rock. Weather-man of the tomb,
We are left among little mice and insects,
Time's clock-work womb.

XIV

Prudence sweetly sang both crotchet and quaver,
Death riped an eyeball, the dog-days
Proffered salt without savour, the cards were cut.
She heard a primordial music, the Host's tune
For the guest's swoon—God going the gamut.
Honour a toast for the regimental mascot,
The thin girl, the boys of the blue fourteenth,
Driving to Ascot: a wedding under the sabres,
Tinker and tailorman, soldier or sailor,
Lads of the village entering harbour,
O respect also those windowless features,
The stainless face of the provincial barber.

Prudence plays monumental patience by candles:
The puffins sit in a book: the muffins are molten:
The crass clock chimes,
Timely the hour and deserved.
Presently will come the two welcome angels
Noise in the hall, the last supper be served.

FIVE SOLILOQUIES UPON THE TOMB
OF UNCEBUNKE

I

My uncle has entered his soliloquy.
He keeps vigil under the black sigil.
To be or not to be at God's suggestion.
That is the question, to know or not to know.

Smoke powder-blue and soft brass handles,
The puma swoons among the silken candles,
O Elsinore, my son, my son,
Tiger of the zenith, heifer of the red herd,
His fugue of flesh and ours in counterpoint,
Which moves, or seems to move.

It is only God's breath in the nave,
Moving the cinquefoils, only the footwork
Of mongols, cretins, and mutes smelling of beer.
(The candles breathe in their pollen)

He that hath ears to hear, let him hear,
Let him bear false witness,
Cough out the candles, covet his neighbour.
Let him crack the ten tablets, burn the puma,
Set up as father, son and ghost,

This, my black humour.

ANTHEM

World without end means voyage beyond feeling.
Trek without turning spells voyage without meaning.
Being, seeing, is voyage at morning.
Dying and praying are travel by kneeling.

II

Friends, Romans, countrymen,
Conduct his entry to soliloquy
With this marginal ritual.
We come to bury Caesar, not to praise him.
God will raise up his bachelor, this widow's mite
A foothold for the scientific worm.

(Deliver us from evil.
Deliver us from the trauma of death's pupil,
From the forked tongue of devil,
Deliver us from the vicar's bubonic purple,
From the canine hysteria, the lethal smile,
O deliver us from botanical sleep,
The canonical sugar, the rabbinical pose,
Deliver us from death's terrific pinnacle,
Biological silence, a clinical sleep.)

This man, my friends,
The lion and the lizard keep,
Mourned by the cottagers on windy porches,
By the cracked hearth-stone, the calendar,
Mourned at the vicarage among the larches:

The shoe full of nails, the ploughboy
Whetting his axe on a bush remembers,
Recalls and regrets: Whom the Gods love
Is death's superlative decoy.

Numen inest. Only the stone puma,
Fluminous under the butter of candles,
Shares this fierce humour.

ANTHEM

Little man's food is brief barley.
His patron is black malt.
Afterwards death is his matron.
Bringing musical bread:
God with his footwork
Bringing musical bread.
Dipped in the heart's dark salt.

III

Friends, Humans, Englishmen!
Officer at the bar and gentleman in bed,
Kings in your counting-houses, clerks at cricket,
All you who play in this desperate game,
Hopes of the side, the tenth wicket,
Who will be certainly raised to the rank of aunt
In the new millennium: permit
The bromoid encomium of the harmonium,
Wear the heart at half-mast and signal
A feudal death of an old order,
The dissolving warrior in his iron hat.

Observe the soul's decorum: stand, my son,
Hymn number one.

ANTHEM

Poor Tom, whose hope was sterile dust
Now perches on an angel's thumb.
While cherubims with silky limbs
Around him hymn and hum.

IV

My uncle has entered his soliloquy;
Under the black sigil the old white one
Kneels in the Lamb's blood,
Hymned by portentous crotchets,
Keeps his smart vigil.

Puma of powder-blue whose stony lip
Reflects the candles, with a mineral eye
Covets the blood, but does not dare to sip.

This man, my Romans, was a Roman,
A breaker of skyline, took first prize
In the regatta for men past menopause,
Passed therough the eye of the needle, broke
The hug of the Great Bear, the hug
Of a glacier's hairy back and oxygen claws.
Spat on Orion, left his shoes in a church,
Hung a harp on every weeping willow,
Took tiffin by the Indian bulrushes, saw
The last deranged crater, swallowed the Word.

Shot his bolt in the Gobi.
Was left in the lurch,
Then like a Roman, fell upon his sword.

This prince, this bug, this human,
Who sleeps under the great cat sleeping,
Shares with the smiling paranoiac,
Shares with the baby in the creeping-suit,
An amniotic balance, the diver's grief.
Has followed a Roman nose past Mandalay,
Ladybird on a leaf.

ANTHEM

Simple addition, simple subtraction.
One is left and the other is taken:
Simple condition but multiple fraction.
One is a doll: the other will waken.
Simple reflection, simple refraction.
Plus or minus, but never just ONE.
Simple equation but multiple action
Ten little nigger boys: now there are none.

V

My uncle has entered his soliloquy.
The candles shed their fur.
O world be nobler for her sake.
The boys hang in the vestry, the days
Are drawing in. Blow out the flesh,
The three-score ten of candles,
This squalid birthday-cake.
Give us to God with slim and shining handles.

All this Peter and Paul knew,
Talked over in the nazarene evenings,
Walked over Galilee arm in arm,
Moved by no wires, by pure imagination.
The prophet who sat under the tall rock
Wrote in a small pure hand this canon
For stockbrokers to read at Cannon Street,
At the Metropole, around the Maypole,
Or smiling in the Ritz: perhaps to endow
An evening conversation at the Plough.

Cousin Judas, let us admit
It is the hour for affirmations,
Let us affirm the no-claim bonus,
The wages of sin, let us admit
Chaos itself as a form of order,
Bear the sinner's pretty onus,
Rediscover the taste of ashes,
Crucify the choirboys: and above all
Preserve the senseless trajectory,
The doom of the bobbin in the loom,
From the rectory to the priory,
From bed to refectory,
From little womb eke to little tomb.

In the name of the Great Whale, then,
Be hale and whole! Amen.

Paris

LETTERS IN DARKNESS

I

So many mockers of the doctrine
Turn away, try not to hear
The antinomian butchers
In the grape-vine of ideas.
It is we who observe who suffer,
We who confide who lie . . .

They are pulling and snapping
The disordered vine-limbs, Dionysus,
The body of our body once divine,
Replacing the coveted order of desire
With all the lumber love can leave,
A star entombed in flesh, desirelessness,
In some ghostly bedroom rented for a night.

II

Connive, Connive,
For the great wheel is turning
Under the politics of the hive.
Connive, for everywhere
Hermits and patron-saints
On the great star-wheel crucified
Pinned out lie burning, burning,
And life is being delivered to the half-alive.

III

Old cock-pheasants when you hit one
Lumber and burst upon the ground,
The body's plump contraption splits
Their lagging rainbow into bits.
So marriage can, by ripeness bound,
From over-ripeness qualify
To sick detachment in the mind—
Dreams bursting at the seams to die
By colder coitus in the mind of God,
Stitches ripped up which used to hold
The modern heart from growing cold.

Now logic founders, speech begins.
Symbols sketch a swaying bridge
Between the states at peace or war,
Athens or Sparta fighting for
What foolish head or fond heart wins.

Much later will the lover coax
Out of the bestiary of his heart
The little hairy sexer, Pan,
The turning-point—pure laughter,
To make the reckoning round and full
If Jill comes tumbling after.
He lies in his love in shadowless content
As tongue in mouth, as poems in a skull.

IV

Jupiter, so lucky when he lay
Trampling among the roses: bodies
Of young girls . . . a cage of sighs
Beside a drifting river-picture
Was all the poet wished in youth
But later saw the glistening dewlap
Of the man-bull, heard the cries,
The squat consorts of the passion
Twisted like figs into the legs
Of washerwomen screeching on the Liffey,
Soaping the flaccid thighs and dugs,
Remagnetized again by thoughts of old
Familiar, incoherent, measureless
Contempts the grabbing flesh must
Always hold, like thefts from human logic,
And savour till the gums and spices fade.

V

Dear, behind the choking estuaries
Of sleep or waking, in the acts
Which dream themselves and make,
Swollen under luminol, responsibilities
Which no one else can take,
I watch the faultless measure of your dying
Into an unknown misused animal
Held by the ropes and drugs; the puny
Recipe society proposes when machines
Break down. Love was our machine.

And through each false connection I
So clearly pierce to reach the God
Infecting this machine, not ours but by
Compulsion of the city and the times;
A God forgetting slowly how to feel:
A broken sex which, lying to itself,
Could never hope to heal.
It was so simple to observe the liars,
The one impaled, and lying like a log,
The other at some fountain-nipple drinking
His art from the whole world, helplessly
Disbanding reason like a thirsty dog.

VI

Madness confides its own theology,
An ape-world bleak in its custom:
Not arbitrary, for even the delusive
Lies concert inside their dissonance:
And are apes less human than
Humans are to each other? Answer.

In clinic beds we reach to where
All cultures intersect, inverted now
By the hungry heart and jumbled out
In friends or sculpture or kissing-stuff,
Measured against the chattering
Of gross primary desires, a code of needs
Where Marxist poems are born and die perhaps.

The white screens they have set up
Like the mind's censor under Babel
Are trying to keep from the white coats

All possible foreknowledge of the enigma.
But the infected face of loneliness
Smiles back wherever mirrors droop and bleed.

VII

Imagine we are the living who inhabit
Freezing offices in a winter town,
Who daily founder deeper in
Our self-disdain being mirrored in
Each others' complicated ways of dying.

Here neither brick nor glass can warm
The sanitary dust of central heating,
And the damp air like a poultice wets
The fears of living which thought begets.

Here we feed, as prisoners feed, spiders
Important to the reason as Bruce's was
Huge sprawling emotions kept in bottles
Below the civil surface of the mind,
That snap and sway upon the webs
Of tearless resignation bought with sleep.

Some few have what I have:
Silent gold pressure of eyes
Belonging to one deeply hurt, deeply aware.
Truly though we never speak
The past has marked us each
In different lives contending for each other:
We bear like ancient marble well-heads
Marks of the ropes they lowered in us,

Telling of the concerns of time,
The knife of feeling in the art of love.

VIII

So at last we come to the writer's
Middle years, the hardest yet to bear,
All will agree: for it is now
He condenses, prunes and tries to order
The experiences which gorged upon his youth.

Every wrinkle now earned is gifted,
Every grey hair tolls. He matches now
Old kisses to new, and in the bodies
Of younger learners throws off his sperm

Like lumber just to ease the weight
Of sighing for their youth, his abandoned own
And in the coital slumber poaches
From lips and tongues the pollen
Of youth, to dust the licence of his art.

You cannot guess how he has been waiting
For these years, these ripe and terrible
Years of the *agon*; with the athlete's
Calm foreknowledge of a deathly ripeness,

Facing perhaps a public death by blows,
Or a massive sprain in the centre of his mind,
The whole world; his champion fever glows
With all the dark misgivings of the bout.

But now even fear cannot despoil the body
And will, trained for the even contest,
Fed by the promise of his country's laurels.

So, having dispossessed himself, and being
Now for the first time prepared to die
He feels at last trained for the second life.

Belgrade

THE PRAYER-WHEEL

Only to affirm in time
That sequence dwells in consequence,
The River's quietly flowing muscle
Turning in the hollow cup
Will teach the human compromise.
Sword and pen win nothing here
Underneath the human floor:
Loved and loving move between
The counterpoint of universes,
Neither less and neither more.

The sage upon his snowy wheel
Secure among the flight of circles
By the calculus of prayer
Underneath the human floor
Founds a commune in the heart.
Time in love's diurnal motion,
Suffering untold migrations,
Islanded and garlanded,
Deep as the ministry of fishes
Lives by a perpetual patience.

Teach us the already known,
Turning in the invisible saucer
By a perfect recreation
Air and water mix and part.
Reaffirm the lover's process,
Faith and love in flesh alloyed,
Spring the cisterns of the heart:
Build the house of entertainment
On the cold circumference
Candle-pointed in the Void.

Cross the threshold of the circle
Turning in its mesmerism
On the fulcrum of the Breath:
Learn the lovely mannerism
Of a perfect art-in-death.
Think: two amateurs in Eden,
Spaces in the voiceless garden,
Ancestors whose haunted faces
Met upon the apple's bruises,
Broke the lovely spell of pardon.

Flower, with your pure assertion,
Mythical and sea-born olive,
Share the indivisible air,
Teach the human compromise:
From a zero, plus or minus,
Born into the great Appearance,
Building cities deep in gardens,
Deeply still the law divines us
In its timeless incoherence.

What is known is never written.
By the equal distribution
He and She and It are genders,
Sparks of carbon on the circle
Meeting in the porch of sex.
Faces mix and numbers mingle
Many aspects of the One
Teach the human compromise.
Speech will never stain the blue,
Nor the lover's occult kisses
Hold the curves of Paradise.

The voices have their dying fall.
The fingers resting on the heart,
The Dumb petitions in the churchyard
Under the European sword
Spell out our tribal suicide.
Grass is green but goes to smoke:
You, my friend, and you, and you,
Breathe on the divining crystal,
Cut down History, the oak:
Prepare us for the sword and pistol.

1939

PARIS JOURNAL

Monday escapes destruction.
Record a vernal afternoon,
Tea on the lawn with mother,
A parochial interest in love, etc.
By the deviation of a hair,
Is death so far, so far, no further.

Tuesday: visibility good: and Wednesday.
A little thunder, some light showers.
A library book about the universe.
The absence of a definite self.
O and already by Friday hazardous,
To Saturday begins the slow reverse.
A Saturday without form. By midnight
The equinox seems forever gone:
Yet the motionless voice repeating:
'Bless the hills in paradigms of smoke,
Manhair, Maidenhair meeting.'

But today Sunday. The pit.
The axe and the knot. Cannot write.
The monster in its booth.
At a quarter to one the mask repeating:
'Truth is what is
Truth is what is Truth?'

COPTIC POEM

A Coptic deputation, going to Ethiopia,
Disappeared up one morning like the ghost in Aubrey

'With a Sweet Odour and a Melodious Twang'.
Who saw them go with their Melodious Odour?

I, said the arrow, the aboriginal arrow,
I saw them go, Coptic and Mellifluous,

Fuzzy-wig, kink-haired, with cocoa-butter shining,
With stoles on poles, sackbuts and silver salvers

Walking the desert ways howling and shining:
A Coptic congregation, red blue and yellow,

With Saints on parchment and stove-pipe hats,
All disappeared up like the ghost in Aubrey

Leaving only a smell of cooking and singing,
Rancid goat-butter and the piss of cats.

MYTHOLOGY

All my favourite characters have been
Out of all pattern and proportion:
Some living in villas by railways,
Some like Katsimbalis heard but seldom seen,
And others in banks whose sunless hands
Moved like great rats on ledgers.

Tibble, Gondril, Purvis, the Duke of Puke,
Shatterblossom and Dude Bowdler
Who swelled up in Jaffa and became a tree:
Hollis who had wives killed under him like horses
And that man of destiny,

Ramon de Something who gave lectures
From an elephant founded a society
To protect the inanimate against cruelty.
He gave asylum to aged chairs in his home,
Lampposts and crockery, everything that
Seemed to him suffering he took in
Without mockery.

The poetry was in the pity. No judgement
Disturbs people like these in their frames
O men of the Marmion class, sons of the free.

POLITICS

Chemists might compare their properties:
The Englishman with his Apologising Bag,
The Ainu with interesting stone-age cuffs,
Or whoever invented stars as a witness:
Nations which through excess of sensibility
Repose in opium under a great leaf:
The French with their elastic manual code:
And so comparing, find the three common desires,
Of hunger, smiling, and of being loved.

Outside, I mean, the penumbra of the real
Mystery, the whole world as a Why.
Living purely in the naked How, so join
As the writer unites dissimilars
Or the doctor with his womb-bag joins
The cumbersome ends of broken bones in
A simple perishable function,
To exhale like a smoke ring the O: Joy.

THE DAILY MIRROR

Writing this stuff should not have been like
Suicide over some ordinary misapprehension:

A man going into his own house, say,
Turning out all the lights before undressing,

At the bedside of some lovely ignoramus
Whispering: 'Tomorrow I swear is the last time.'

Or: 'Believe, and I swear you will never die.'
This nib dragged out like the late train

Racing on iron bars for the north.
Target: another world, not necessarily better,

Of course, but different, completely different.
The hour-glass shifting its trash of seconds.

If it does not end this way perhaps some other.
Gossip lying in a furnished room, blinds drawn.

A poem with its throat cut from ear to ear.

PRESSMARKED URGENT

'Mens sana in corpore sano'—*Motto for Press Corps*

DESPATCH ADGENERAL PUBLICS EXTHE WEST
PERPETUAL MOTION QUITE UNFINDING REST
ADVANCES ETRETREATS UPON ILLUSION
PREPARES NEW METAPHYSICS PERCONFUSION

PARA PERDISPOSITION ADNEW EVIL
ETREFUSAL ADCONCEDE OUR ACTS ADDEVIL
NEITHER PROFIT SHOWS NOR LOSS
SEDSOME MORE PROPHETS NAILED ADCROSS

ATTACK IN FORCE SURMEANS NONENDS
BY MULTIPLYING CONFUSION TENDS
ADCLOUD THE ISSUES WHICH ARE PLAIN
COLON DISTINGUISH PROFIT EXGAIN

ETBY SMALL CONCEPTS LONG NEGLECTED
FIND VIRTUE SUBACTION CLEAR REFLECTED
ETWEIGHING THE QUANTUM OF THE SIN
BEGIN TO BE REPEAT BEGIN.

ELEGY ON THE CLOSING OF THE FRENCH BROTHELS

(For Henry Miller and George Katsimbalis)

I

Last of the great autumnal capitals
Disengaging daily like a sword
The civil codes, behaviour, friendship, love,
In houses of shining glass,
On tablecloths stained with pools of light,
By the rambling river's evening scents
Carried our freight of pain so lightly:
And towards evening when the inkwells overturn
And at last the figure which has sat
Motionless for hours, pours himself out
One glass of moonlight, drinks it, and retires.

By the railway arches a stone plinth.
Under the shadows of the lamps the figures.
So many ways of dividing up the self:
Correspondences moving outwards along a line
Of nerves, the memory of letters
Smelling like apples in an empty cupboard,
And at midnight the pall of clocks,
At odds among themselves, the shuffling
Of innumerable packs of cards where each shall see
One day his face instead of fortune's be.

Bound here to the great axis of the sex,
Black source that feeds your manners, gives
Information and vivacity to food and linen,
Determined as the penetration into self-abuse—
For each separation by kisses forges new bonds:
Three or four words on the back of a letter,
Tessa waiting on a corner with all she feels,
Rain glittering in that peacock's eye,
As heavy with sense as a king's letter with seals.

Here the professional observer met you,
The amateur in melancholy,
To the swish of an invisible fountain,
Drinking from a glass under a man on horseback,
Talking to a lady with a poisoned finger.

Women turned over by the mind and each
A proper noun, an act of trespass,
Improper for its aberration but accepted
As in a mirror one is twice but accepts.
So in these magazines of love they moved,
Experience misbegotten in each face like rings
In wood, were commentators on our weakness,
Through cycles of repentance in the blood,
Exhausted the body's ugly contents in a sigh,
Left, hard as ash, the object's shape: an art
Eros began, self-murder carries on.

III

Of all the sicknesses, autumnal Paris,
This self-infection was the best, where friends
Like self-possession could be learned
Through the mystery of a slit
Like a tear in an old fur coat,
A hole in a paper lantern where the seeing I
Looked out and measured one:
The ferocious knuckle of a sex
Standing to acknowledge like a hambone
Our membership in the body of a tribe
Holy and ridiculous at once:
Symbol of unrecognised desire, pain, pain.

You might have seen silence flower in eyes,
The tobacco eyes of every human critic,
Or a mouth laid along the meniscus
Of a lighted glass blazing like a diamond.

All the great brothels closed save Sacré Coeur!
Windows boarded up from the inheritors,
The nameless donors inhabiting marble fanes
On peninsulas with cocks of gold in sunlight,
Under the oleanders, printed in warm moss,
The bare ankles playing on a flute,
Selecting the bodies of boys, the temporary
Refuge for a kiss on the silver backs of mirrors:
Powder of statues in a grove born old,
Born sightless, wingless, never to be loved.

Crude man in his coat of nerves and hair
Whose kisses like apostles go about
On translated business never quite his own,
Derives from the obscure medium of the body,
As through some glass coffin, a retrievéd sprite,
Himself holding the holy bottle, fast asleep.

All these rotten galleries were symbols
Of us, where the girls like squirrels
Leaned in the tarnished mirrors sadly sighing:
The wind in empty clothing, while the destroyer
Sorted the bottles for just the right medicine.

Below us, far below on the stairway somewhere
Tessa had already combed the dark disorder
Of curls, the flash of pectorals in a mirror,
Invented already this darker niece of Egypt,
Who leaves the small hashish-pipe by the pillow,
Uneasy in red slippers like the dust in urns,
The smashed columns, wells full of leaves,
The faces white as burns.

V

We suffer according to the terms we make
With time in cities: allowing to be rooted from us
Like useless teeth the few great healers
Who understand the penalties of confession,
And cannot fear these half-invented Gods,
Inhabiting our own cities of unconquered pain.

Now the capitals settle slowly in the sea
Of their failures. All the common brute has done
Building like a rat the rotten shanties
Of his self-esteem beside the water's edge,
His fear and prejudice into a dead index.
It is not enough. We have still to outgrow
The prohibitions in us with the fears they grow from:
For the beloved will be no happier
Nor the unloved less hungry when the miracle begins:
Yet both will be ineffably disclosed
In their own natures by simplicity
Like roses in a giving off of grace.

THE CRITICS

They never credit us
With being bad enough
The boys that come to edit us:
Of simply not caring when a prize,
Something for nothing, comes our way,
A wife, a mistress, or a holiday
From People living neckfast in their lies.

No: Shakespear's household bills
Could never be responsible, they say,
For all the heartbreak and the 1,000 ills
His work is heir to, poem, sonnet, play . . .
Emended readings give the real reason:
The times were out of joint, the loves, the season.

Man With A Message—how could you forget
To read your proofs, the heartache and the fret?
The copier or the printer
Must take the blame for it in all
The variants they will publish by the winter.

'By elision we quarter suffering.' Too true.
'From images and scansion can be learned.' . . .
Yet under it perhaps may be discerned
A something else afoot—a Thing
Lacking both precedent and name and gender:
An uncreated Weight which left its clue,
Making him run up bills,
Making him violent or distrait or tender:
Leaving for Stratford might have heard It say:
'Tell them I won't be back on Saturday.
My wife will understand I'm on a bender.'

And to himself muttering, muttering: 'Words
Added to words multiply the space
Between this feeling and my expressing It.
The wires get far too hot. Time smoulders
Like a burning rug. I *will* be free.' . . .

And all the time from the donkey's head
The lover is whispering: 'This is not
What I imagined as Reality.
If truth were needles surely eyes would see?'

MYTHOLOGY

Miss Willow, secretly known as 'tit' . . .
Plotkin who slipped on new ice
And wounded the stinks master
The winter when the ponds froze over . . .

Square roots of the symbol Abraham
Cut off below the burning bush,
Or in the botany classes heads
Drying between covers like rare ferns,
Stamen and pistil, we were young then.

Later with tunes like 'Hips and Whores'
The song-book summed us up,
Mixing reality with circumstance,
With Hotchkiss cock of the walk
Top button undone, and braided cap,
He was the way and the life.

What dismays is not time
Assuaging every thirst with a surprise,
Bitterness hidden in desiring bodies,
Unfolded strictly, governed by the germ.

Plotkin cooked like a pie in iron lungs:
Glass rods the doctors dipped in burning nitrates
Dripped scalding on in private hospitals
And poor 'tit' Willow who had been
Young, pretty and perhaps contemptuous
Dreaming of love, was carried to Spain in a cage.

SONG FOR ZARATHUSTRA

Le saltimbanque is coming with
His heels behind his head.
His smile is mortuary and
His whole expression dead.

The acrobat, the acrobat,
Demanding since the Fall
Little enough but hempen stuff
To climb and hang us all.

Mysterious inventions like
The trousers and the hat
Bewitched our real intentions:
We sewed the fig-leaves flat.

Man sewed his seven pockets
Upon his hairy clothes
But woman in her own white flesh
Has one she seldom shows.

An aperture on anguish,
A keyhole on disgrace:
The features stay grimacing
Upon the mossy face.

A cup without a handle
A staff without a crook,
The sawdust in the golly's head,
The teapot with the nook.

The Rib is slowly waking
Within the side of Man
And *le guignol* is making
Its faces while it can.

Compose us in the finder
Our organs upside down,
The parson in his widow's weeds,
The doctor in his gown.

What Yang and Yin divided
In one disastrous blunder
Must one day be united and
Let no man put asunder.

BALLAD OF KRETSCHMER'S TYPES

(pyknics are short, fat and hairy,
leptosomes thin and tall)

The schizophrene, the cyclothyme
Swerve from the droll to the sublime,
Coming of epileptoid stock
They tell the time without a clock.

The pyknic is the prince of these
And glorifies his mental status
Not by acts on mind's trapeze
But purely by divine afflatus.

Oblivious to the critic's canon
The rational booby's false décor
He swigs away the Absolute
And then demands some more.

Pity the lanky leptosome
Myoptic tenebrous and glum
Whose little pigs must stay at home
Unless they move by rule of thumb.

Salute the podgling pyknic then
That gross and glabrous prince of men,
Contriver of the poet's code
And hero of the Comic Mode.

And Lord, condemn the leptosome
To Golgotha his natural home
The pyknic who's half saint half brute
O waft him on Thy parachute,
And may his footsteps ever roam
Where alcohol is Absolute.

BALLAD OF THE OEDIPUS COMPLEX

From Travancore to Tripoli
I trailed the great Imago,
Wherever Freud has followed me
I felt Mama and Pa go.

(The engine loves the driver
And the driver loves his mate,
The mattress strokes the pillow
And the pencil pokes the slate)

I tried to strangle it one day
While sitting in the Lido
But it got up and tickled me
And now I'm all Libido.

My friends spoke to the Censor
And the censor warned the Id
By though they tried to hush things up
They neither of them did.

(The barman loves his potion
And the admiral his barge,
The frogman loves the ocean
And the soldier his discharge.)

(The critic loves urbanity
The plumber loves his tool.
The preacher all humanity
The poet loves the fool.)

271

If seven psychoanalysts
On seven different days
Condemned my coloured garters
Or my neo-Grecian stays,

I'd catch a magic constable
And lock him behind bars
To be a warning to all men
Who have mamas and pas.

A BALLAD OF THE GOOD LORD NELSON

The Good Lord Nelson had a swollen gland,
Little of the scripture did he understand
Till a woman led him to the promised land
    Aboard the Victory, Victory O.

Adam and Evil and a bushel of figs
Meant nothing to Nelson who was keeping pigs,
Till a woman showed him the various rigs
    Aboard the Victory, Victory O.

His heart was softer than a new laid egg,
Too poor for loving and ashamed to beg,
Till Nelson was taken by the Dancing Leg
    Aboard the Victory, Victory O.

Now he up and did up his little tin trunk
And he took to the ocean on his English junk,
Turning like the hour-glass in his lonely bunk
    Aboard the Victory, Victory O.

The Frenchman saw him a-coming there
With the one-piece eye and the valentine hair,
With the safety-pin sleeve and occupied air
    Aboard the Victory, Victory O.

Now you all remember the message he sent
As an answer to Hamilton's discontent—
There were questions asked about it in Parliament
    Aboard the Victory, Victory O.

Now the blacker the berry, the thicker comes the juice.
Think of Good Lord Nelson and avoid self-abuse,
For the empty sleeve was no mere excuse
    Aboard the Victory, Victory O.

'England Expects' was the motto he gave
When he thought of little Emma out on Biscay's wave,
And remembered working on her like a galley-slave
    Aboard the Victory, Victory O.

The first Great Lord in our English land
To honour the Freudian command,
For a cast in the bush is worth two in the hand
    Aboard the Victory, Victory O.

Now the Frenchman shot him there as he stood
In the rage of battle in a silk-lined hood
And he heard the whistle of his own hot blood
    Aboard the Victory, Victory O.

Now stiff on a pillar with a phallic air
Nelson stylites in Trafalgar Square
Reminds the British what once they were
    Aboard the Victory, Victory O.

If they'd treat their women in the Nelson way
There'd be fewer frigid husbands every day
And many more heroes on the Bay of Biscay
    Aboard the Victory, Victory O.

BALLAD OF PSYCHOANALYSIS

Monday

She dreams she is chased by a black buck-nigger
But a fall in the coal-face blocks out the dream,
Something as long and lank as a lanyard,
Slow as a glacier, cold as cold cream—
Something inside her starts to scream . . .

Tuesday

Dreams she is chased by a man in a nightshirt,
Lawrence of Arabia dressed in a sheet:
Then locked by the crew of a Liberty Ship
With rows and rows and rows of refrigerated meat
While the voices keep repeating 'Eat'.

Wednesday

Dreams she is handcuffed to a dancing-partner
And dragged round a roller-skating rink.
She swallows the ring on her wedding-finger
Falls through the ice but doesn't seem to sink
Though her party clothes begin to shrink.

Thursday

Dreams she is queen of a mountain of cork,
Too hot to sit on, too cold to wear,
Naked, she pricks with a toasting-fork
A statue of Venus reclining there
With a notice saying: No charge for wear and tear.

275

Friday

She dreams she's a dog-team tugging poor Scott,
Sheer to the confines of the Pole:
Suddenly the Arctic becomes a-burning hot,
And when they arrive it's just an empty hole,
A geyser whistling in a mountain of coal.

Saturday

Dreams she's the queen of a city-culture
Lovely as Helen but doomed to spoil:
Under her thighs roll the capital rivers,
The Rhine and the Volga flowing like oil.
Hamlet offers her a buttoned foil.

Sunday

What has she got that we haven't got?
Isn't she happy and lovely too?
She dreams that her husband a bank-director
Locked in the Monkey-House at the Zoo—
Here's the clinical picture but what can we do?

DEUS LOCI

I

All our religions founder, you
remain, small sunburnt *deus loci*
safe in your natal shrine,
landscape of the precocious southern heart,
continuously revived in passion's common
tragic and yet incorrigible spring:
in every special laughter overheard,
your specimen is everything—
accents of the little cackling god,
part animal, part insect, and part bird.

II

This dust, this royal dust, our mother
modelled by spring-belonging rain
whose soft blank drops console
a single vineyard's fever or a region
falls now in soft percussion on the earth's
old stretched and wrinkled vellum skin:
each drop could make one think
a footprint of the god, but out of season,
yet in your sudden coming know
life lives itself without recourse to reason.

III

On how many of your clement springs
the fishermen set forth, the foresters
resign their empty glasses, rise,
confront the morning star, accept
the motiveless patronage of all you are—
desire recaptured on the sea or land
in the fables of fish, or grapes held up,
a fistful of some champion wine
glowing like a stained-glass window
in a drunkard's trembling hand.

IV

All the religions of the dust can tell—
this body of damp clay that cumbered so
Adam, and those before, was given him,
material for his lamp and spoon and body
to renovate your terra cotta shrines
whose cupids unashamed
to make a fable of the common lot
curled up like watchsprings in a kiss,
or turned to *putti* for a lover's bed,
or *amorini* for a shepherd's little cot.

V

Known before the expurgation of gods
wherever nature's carelessness exposed
her children to the fear of the unknown—

in families gathered by hopeless sickness
about a dying candle, or in sailors
on tilting decks and under shrouded planets:
wherever the unknown has displaced the known
you encouraged in the fellowship of wine
of love and husbandry: and in despair
only to think of you and you were there.

VI

The saddle-nose, the hairy thighs
composed these vines, these humble vines,
so dedicated to themselves yet offering
in the black froth of grapes their increment
to pleasure or to sadness where a poor
peasant at a husky church-bell's chime
crosses himself: on some cracked pedestal
by the sighing sea sets eternally up,
item by item, his small mid-day meal,
garlic and bread, the wine-can and the cup.

VII

Image of our own dust in wine!
drinkers of that royal dust pressed out
drop by cool drop in science and in love
into a model of the absconding god's
image—human like our own. Or else in other
mixtures, of breath in kisses dropped
under the fig's dark noonday lantern, yes,
lovers like tenants of a wishing-well
whose heartbeats labour through all time has stopped.

VIII

Your panic fellowship is everywhere,
Not only in love's first great illness known,
but in the exile of objects lost
to context, broken hearts, spilt milk,
oaths disregarded, laws forgotten:
or on the seashore some old pilot's
capital in rags of sail, snapped oars,
water-jars choked with sand,
and further on, half hidden, the fatal letter
in the cold fingers of some marble hand.

IX

Deus loci your provinces extend
throughout the domains of logic,
beyond the eyes watching from dusty murals,
or the philosopher's critical impatience
to understand, to be done with life:
beyond beyond even the mind's dark spools
in a vine-wreath or an old wax cross
you can become the nurse and wife of fools,
their actions and their nakedness—
all the heart's profit or the loss.

X

So today, after many years, we meet
at this high window overlooking
the best of Italy, smiling under rain,

that rattles down the leaves like sparrow-shot,
scatters the reapers, the sunburnt girls,
rises in the sour dust of this table,
these books, unfinished letters—all
refreshed again in you O spirit of place,
Presence long since divined, delayed, and waited for,
And here met face to face.

Forio d'Ischia

INDEX OF FIRST LINES

284

287